FOREIGN POLICY WITHOUT FEAR

Foreign Policy without Fear

VERA MICHELES DEAN

McGraw-Hill Book Company, Inc.

NEW YORK   TORONTO   LONDON

FOREIGN POLICY WITHOUT FEAR

To WILLIAM EMERY NICKERSON
*one of the best of Americans who by making me the
gift of an American education taught me
the best of America*

PREFACE

A PERIOD of tumultuous flux like the one in which we are living poses grave problems for the government officials who must make policy decisions. For if the American people are led to feel that these officials have failed, as on the question of policy toward China, the verdict will be: "Off with their heads" — figuratively, at least.

This period also poses soul-searching problems for the contemporary historian whose diagnosis of the situation, however indirectly, may influence public opinion and thus be reflected in policy. For obviously the wrong diagnosis could in this age of atomic warfare bring about incalculable catastrophe.

The historian finds himself in a practically untenable position. At best, he sees only the tip of the iceberg of events, the bulk of which is concealed below the surface of documents classified as secret. The best the expert can do is to work like an Impressionist painter, putting down on paper the impressions he has of world affairs in his own times. But no matter how much he strives, with utmost integrity, to describe events as they appear to him, the same events appear quite different to others, onlookers or participants, who do not hesitate to accuse him of bias or myopia. The role of the expert is curiously ill-defined in the United States. He is apparently expected not merely to report what he sees, to the best of his ability, but also to act as prophet — and then if changing events over which he has no control do not conform to the views he expressed ten or twenty years before, he becomes an object of public abuse such as was once reserved for hardened criminals.

An interpreter of the past may face predicaments comparable in kind — obviously there is more than one interpretation of the fall of Rome, the Napoleonic conquests, or the effects of the French Revolution — but not in the immediacy of impact on his own existence. For contemporaries who passionately differ with him concerning events which they, too, have an opportunity to observe may, as we have seen in our own time, traduce him publicly and deprive him of livelihood on charges of subversion or treason. Yet the historian who, out of anxiety about his personal interests, capitulates to public clamor and becomes a mere recorder of the most popular interpretation placed on current events is the one really guilty of betrayal. He betrays the trust placed in him as the appraiser — not wholly dispassionate, since man can never be a mere calculating machine, but striving for dispassionateness — of events analyzed in the perspective of history.

But in the life-and-death struggle of empires and ideas the historian is summoned by his fellow men to take sides, to pronounce himself, not merely to record. Yet the moment he does so he properly loses his claim to Olympian detachment; he becomes, and is praised or denounced, as a partisan. He is urged to depict "reality." He is warned against cherishing "illusions" — illusions about democracy, or communism, or international cooperation, or isolationism, as the case may be. He becomes engulfed in somewhat the same controversy as has been rending the world of art and the world of science — the controversy between the "realists" and the "abstractionists." What is the truth in contemporary events? Are all those who differ from us in our views of the world mistaken individuals whom we must endeavor to enlighten — or are they scoundrels beyond our power to reform whom we should verbally destroy? Do all heretics genuinely see things differently from us — or are they willfully spreading lies about their concepts of the universe?

The exchange of views in August 1951 between Viscount Samuel of Britain and Dr. Albert Einstein about contemporary physics has a poignant relevance for the historian. To Viscount Samuel's charge that "contemporary physics are based on concepts somewhat analogous to the 'smile' of the absent cat,' " Dr. Einstein replied: "The real is in no way immediately given to us. Given to us are merely the data of our consciousness. . . . There is only one way from the data of consciousness to 'reality,' to wit, the way of conscious or unconscious intellectual construction, which proceeds completely free and arbitrarily. . . . One is in danger of being misled by the illusion that the real of our daily experience 'exists really' and that certain concepts of physics are 'mere ideas' separated from the 'real' by an unbridgeable gulf." Dr. Einstein places more trust in the "real" which is arrived at as a result of intellectual construction than in that which appears "real" because it stands in a correspondence with our sensations. "These facts could be expressed in a paradox," he holds, "namely that 'reality' as we know it is exclusively composed of 'fancies.' " Speaking of scientists, he says: "We are free to choose which elements we wish to apply in our construction of physical reality. The justification of our choice lies exclusively in our success."

Like the scientist, the historian, too, must make a choice of those elements of reality in contemporary events which to him seem particularly significant, and must place them in the relation to each other which, in his judgment, appears most accurate.

The making of these choices is a grave, an onerous, responsibility. Unlike the scientist, the historian is not in a position to subject his conclusions to the concrete test of laboratory experiments. His success or failure cannot be measured with exactitude in charts or statistical tables. Only the actual trend of public affairs can demonstrate whether or not his choices were justified; and by the very nature of things such justification may not be forthcoming in his lifetime. To an even greater extent than the scientist, therefore, the historian must be willing to take full responsibility for his interpretation of the contemporary world — for such distinctions as he draws between realities and myths.

This task is particularly harrowing in a period of profound upheavals, when the contenders for material power and ideological influence understandably seek to bolster their claims with impassioned assertions on behalf of their own beliefs and achievements and equally impassioned denigration of the beliefs and achievements of their opponents. As has been discovered by all those who are engaged in forming public opinion, there is hardly any situation or idea, no matter how unrelated to reality, which cannot be made to appear real in people's minds by sufficient reiteration. This is true not only in countries like nazi Germany or communist Russia, where a totalitarian state controls all channels of communication; but, as we have learned from our own experience here in the past few years, myths can be created even in a society which offers opportunities for free discussion. Even the historian, either through deference to public opinion or out of the sheer fatigue of resisting popularly accepted slogans, is apt to succumb to the reiterative process and stop trying to ascertain whether there may be another side to the official picture or possible alternatives to current policies.

But the historian who abdicates his capacity to diagnose events really surrenders his function both as a student and as a citizen in a free society. If he wants to live at peace with his conscience, he must continue to speak his mind as long as the opportunity to do so exists. For his role is not merely to list events, but to try and interpret them — let the chips fall where they may.

VERA MICHELES DEAN

New York City
February 21, 1953

CONTENTS

"Everybody's friend is everybody's fool."

LILLI PALMER

*"If I knew what I was afraid of I wouldn't
be frightened."* GIOVANNI GUARESCHI
*The Little World of Don
Camillo*

I

THE REALITIES OF
WORLD AFFAIRS

THE new Administration which took office in January 1953
had, as one of its first tasks, to reexamine the foreign policy
of the United States and to review the far-flung commitments
made by this country abroad since 1945.

It is quite true, as some opponents of the Truman Administration said during the presidential campaign, that the United
States often resorted to improvisation during the postwar years.
This happened, in part, because Americans — Republicans as
well as Democrats — were new to the tasks of international
statesmanship and, finding themselves suddenly and reluctantly
thrust into the center of the world stage, literally had to improvise their lines from one crisis to another. In part, also, this was
due to the prevailing assumption, held by Republicans and
Democrats alike, that the United States faced a short-term
emergency in world affairs and that, once the emergency had
been met by an all-out military and economic effort, we would
be able to relax and go about our normal business.

Now we know that we must face a long-term situation from
which there is no easy exit. Henceforth we must calculate and
plan, not merely improvise in piecemeal fashion. And we must
plan on the basis of things as they are, not as we would like
them to be. Nor will it help us, or the rest of the world, to keep

on chewing and rechewing the cud of old grievances and stale regrets over what we or someone else did or left undone. It is essential for the morale of the American people that we shake off the fears which have assailed us in the postwar years and have often beclouded our judgment and, instead of brooding on the past, begin to draw up blueprints for the future.

For two bitter years, since the United States decided to resist aggression in South Korea on behalf of the United Nations, we have been in the grip of a violent debate about the objectives and methods of this country's foreign policy. This debate reached a dramatic climax during the presidential campaign when Gen. Dwight D. Eisenhower, who had played a major and much admired part in implementing the Democratic Administration's policy in Europe, asserted that the "containment" of Russia and communism, initiated by President Truman in 1947, had proved a failure, and called for a new positive approach through the "liberation" of all peoples in Europe and Asia held captive by the U.S.S.R. When chided by President Truman, who contended that "liberation" would involve the risk of atomic war, General Eisenhower and other Republican spokesmen answered that their goal could be achieved by peaceful means, through the encouragement of passive resistance and sabotage in the satellite countries and more effective propaganda from the United States.

Critics of the Truman Administration have argued that the U.S.S.R. would never have gained the territories and influence it now commands in Europe and Asia if it had not been for the weaknesses, mistakes, and, in some instances, outright betrayal of American interests by the Roosevelt and Truman governments during the war and after, from Teheran and Yalta to Korea and Formosa. They have declared that by "appeasing" the Kremlin at a time when the United States and Russia were fighting the same enemy, and then by acquiescing in Russia's postwar moves until the Czechoslovak coup of 1947, the Administration made it possible for the Soviet government to capture control of eighteen countries, including China, and thus helped to enhance the power of the U.S.S.R. and gravely imperiled the security of the United States and the rest of the free world. According to the critics, the decision of President Truman in 1947 to "contain" Russia by a series of measures ranging from aid to Greece and Turkey and the Marshall Plan to the Point Four program of 1949 and United Nations intervention in Korea in 1950, came too late after the event to undo the harm wrought during the war and the early postwar period. By that time, as they see it, the U.S.S.R. had become so entrenched that the United States and its allies could do no more than hold the line against the farther expansion of Russia and communism along a far-flung periphery, at a high cost in lives, money, and materials, but with no hope of ousting Russia from the positions it had gained or of restoring the freedom of the peoples conquered by the Kremlin and bringing them back into the orbit of the non-communist world.

Under these circumstances, the critics went on, the United States would be indefinitely committed to a program which might not only exhaust its resources, and thus bring about the economic collapse predicted by Soviet leaders, but also promised nothing to the American people and our allies except frustration and disappointment. "Containment," in their opinion, was both inconclusive abroad and demoralizing for Americans who were made to feel that they should supinely tolerate the enslavement of other nations rather than fight, as became their tradition, for moral principles. Instead of merely containing Russia, and thereby, by implication, acquiescing in its conquests, the United States, they urged, should turn to a dynamic policy of liberation which would give fresh hope and encouragement not only to Americans but to all peoples, including those of the U.S.S.R.

To this growing demand for the abandonment of "con-

tainment" in favor of "liberation," spokesmen for the Truman
Administration, notably Secretary of State Dean Acheson, replied by pointing out that the United States could not embark on a positive policy until it had achieved "situations of
strength" on which it could base a new positive approach to
conflicts between the non-communist world and Russia. The
policy of containment, according to these spokesmen, had
succeeded in its main purpose — that of preventing further
significant expansion of Russian and communist influence. Except in Korea, this purpose had been achieved without resort
to force, through military, economic, and diplomatic aid to
nations threatened by Russian encroachments. The Truman
Administration did not differ with its critics about the desirability of liberating the peoples held captive by the U.S.S.R.,
and had in fact used both encouragement to underground
movements and propaganda to keep the flame of resistance
alive in the satellite countries. It took the view, however, that
liberation at the present stage of world affairs would precipitate a world conflict, and since both sides in the cold war now
have atomic bombs, this would mean the threat of an atomic
collision which might obliterate captors, captives, and liber-
ators alike.

Instead, the Truman Administration continued to hope
that the patient building-up of military strength by the non-
communist world sufficient to avert aggression by Russia, and
a parallel program for the improvement of political, economic,
and social conditions in nations outside Russia's orbit sufficient
to avert the further spread of communism, would ultimately
place the United States in a position where it might effectively
negotiate with Russia. Even if the American people should
choose liberation by force in preference to the continuance
of "containment," the United States, which relies on the support of allies in Europe and Asia and on the collective security
system of the United Nations, would not find it possible "to

go it alone" against the U.S.S.R. This country, therefore, in the opinion of the Truman Administration's policy makers, must arm itself with patience for a long-drawn-out cold war, and avoid rash gestures and promises that might cause the Soviet leaders to regard the defensive preparations of the non-communist world as preparations for a "preventive" war.

It is perfectly understandable that the American people, disheartened and frustrated by two years of seemingly fruitless war and truce negotiations in Korea, should want to "fish or cut bait." At the present time, however, the majority of our people are not prepared to accept the logical conclusions either of the "containment" policy developed by the Democratic Administration and hitherto supported by many Republicans, or of the "liberation" policy urged by its Republican critics. As spokesmen for the Truman Administration have frequently stated, "containment" is not regarded as an end in itself, but as a shield behind which the non-communist world can build sufficient military and economic power to negotiate with Russia from "strength." Yet there is little disposition in the United States to welcome the prospect of global negotiations such as Moscow has suggested. There has been practically no discussion here about the conditions Washington would expect the U.S.S.R. to accept in Europe and Asia if a conference were held, and the prevailing distrust of the Kremlin, strengthened by Moscow's "hate" campaign in 1952, raise serious doubts about the reliability of any promise Russia might make. Until the international atmosphere improves — and, in the absence of unforeseen events, this may take years — "containment," at best, offers a relatively bearable method of maintaining the existing balance of power and, at worst, an opportunity to build up the military strength of the non-communist world in case Russia upsets this balance by resorting to aggression.

By contrast, a policy of "liberation" might create the risk

of hot war with Russia and of an expanded war with the Chinese Communists, assuming that China is to be included among the countries to be liberated. Yet there is no indication at the present time that a majority of the American people favor war outside of Korea, where, it is still earnestly hoped, a truce may eventually be reached. If, however, the new Administration should devise means of achieving liberation without resort to war, the United States would still have to decide what conditions it could offer the satellite countries to assure them that once they have regained their freedom they can hope to enjoy a modicum of economic well-being and of security from attack by great-power neighbors.

Thus in either case, whether "containment" is continued or "liberation" is attempted, the American people will have to undertake a searching reassessment of the problems it faces in the second half of the twentieth century, and of the alternative courses it might follow. Coming with little advance preparation to its new role of leadership in world affairs, the United States has understandably found itself immersed in many difficulties. The most fundamental of these difficulties, and one which we are only beginning to overcome, is that many of us, as John Cogley of the Catholic journal, *The Commonweal*, has put it, are "either not ready, or not willing, to deal with the realities of the times." Some of us still look back with nostalgia to isolation, and bitterly resent every move toward international action, while at the same time criticizing anyone who does not continuously denounce Russia and communism. Others, who regard international cooperation as the only course open to the United States, are not satisfied with the limited results achieved thus far, and demand Utopia, but often without any desire to make the adjustments in personal and national interests which a utopian program would require. Dreams of one kind or another, about the past or the future, are substituted for the realities of the present, and an attempt, doomed to failure, is then made to translate these dreams into terms of policy.

A nation like the United States which, as the report of the Paley Committee pointed out in 1952, depends increasingly on imports of raw materials from all quarters of the globe for the continuance of its economic activities and, because of its high degree of industrial concentration, is now peculiarly vulnerable to atomic warfare, which it has helped to develop, cannot hope to return to isolation. We need the rest of the world just as they need us. Cooperation with other countries that can provide us with markets for our goods, raw materials for our industries, strategic bases, military aid, and moral support, is not a matter of altruism on our part. It is a matter of necessity for national survival.

Nor is the United States, even though it is today potentially the most powerful nation in the world — a fact which the Russians would be the first to admit — in a position to dictate the conduct of other countries, even if it wanted to do so. In the United Nations we are working with many nations that, no matter how friendly to the United States, would turn away from us if they thought that we were trying to impose our will on them. It is impossible for us to make the United Nations an instrument for carrying out our policies, no matter how wise and necessary those policies may seem to us. We have to use persuasion, not coercion, if we are to win and keep friends in this international forum. Thus neither the alternative of isolation nor that of an American-dictated Utopia is open to the United States. The road open to us is a middle road of working with other nations to the fullest extent of our ability but without expecting that every objective dear to our hearts will be promptly and unqualifiedly achieved.

What are the realities of world affairs? Because of our previous invulnerability to attack, the United States had never had to experience, until now, the anxieties and dangers which other nations have known for centuries. Not unnaturally, the international and civil wars of our times have seemed to us to be *sui generis,* and our enemies — first German nazism and Japanese totalitarian militarism, then Russian communism — assumed for us the aspect of demonic forces never before witnessed by mankind.

The belief that we were engaged in mortal combat not with nations and ideological movements led by men but with some kind of evil spirits made us willing to undertake a moral crusade which an old-fashioned struggle for power could not have inspired. The trouble with the crusading approach to world affairs, however, is that once the demons have been exorcised — as after the unconditional surrender of the Germans and the Japanese — and it becomes apparent that the world continues to be plagued by many troubles, then the danger arises that we may simply throw up our hands in despair at human wickedness. At that point, since return to old-style isolationism is precluded by air warfare reinforced by atomic bombs and even more deadly new weapons, the United States, our friends fear, may revert instead to the course followed by other great powers in history and use vastly increased armaments to impose on the world the way of life it regards as just. This fear was strengthened in 1951 by the statements of General of the Army Douglas MacArthur who, far from being an isolationist of *The Chicago Tribune* type, was regarded as the chief proponent of isolated interventionism, of "going it alone" with no regard for the interests or objections of our allies — in short, of nineteenth-century imperialism in the atomic age.

Actually the divergence between the United States and other non-communist nations in their interpretation of the character, dangers, and promises of our times is one of degree rather than of essence. During the interwar years many countries now regarded by us as being "on our side" were far more clearly aware than the United States of the dangers of German nazism, Italian fascism, and Japanese militant totalitarianism, but at that time their Cassandra warnings left most of us unmoved, and brought no action on our part until the witches' caldron had boiled over in Europe and Asia. Today these countries do not quarrel with our forebodings, reminiscent of their own in the 1930s — this time about the dangers of Russia and communism. They agree that an aggressive Russia, armed with all the dread attributes of the police state and Communist parties in other nations subservient to Moscow's aims, threatens the security and freedoms of the Western world as well as the independence of new nations that, though lacking the political traditions of the West, are nevertheless determined to resist Russian encroachments and communist subversion. But none of our actual or would-be allies — not even Franco Spain — see Russia and communism in exactly the same focus as we do. To us, first Hitler and the Japanese, now Russia and the Communists, are not merely new aspirants to world power, but possess an evil quality so much outside the range of our practical experience that we tend to explain it in superhuman, or subhuman, terms, not in relation to other events in history.

Confronted unexpectedly with the need to assume a position of leadership after the war in the midst of one of the most revolutionary periods of modern times, we have allowed ourselves to become beset with fear born out of uncertainty, and have come to view events as wholly black or white, with no intermediate shades in between. Our national tendency to moralize — a tendency we share with the British — has caused us to see the world not in terms of geography, economics, military strategy, social clashes, and so on, but as a sort of Zoroastrian struggle between good and evil, between the virtuous West and the nefarious Russians (and only yesterday the Germans and Japanese). This division of the universe into watertight moral compartments has made it more and more difficult for us to look straightforwardly and calmly at the facts of international life. Animated by fear of communism, we have increasingly countered Russia's rigid dogmas with rigid dogmas of our own. And at times we have arrived at a dissociation between reality and our interpretation of reality — a dissociation which has not only widened the already wide gulf between us and the Russians but, more important, has caused some of our staunchest supporters in other countries to doubt the accuracy of our vision.

Let us look at some of our assumptions about world affairs and how these assumptions appear to other peoples who are friendly to the United States.

Americans have been brought up to believe that the concept of balance of power between nations is inherently evil. This concept, it was once thought among Americans, was devised by the British to maintain their position of preeminence first on the European continent and then on the world scene. Because of this belief, we have been profoundly opposed to such corollaries of the balance of power as spheres of influence, special trade arrangements, strategic bases in other countries, and so on. We have expected all nations, great and small, to act from altruistic motives rather than to advance their own interests, and to leave each other alone except in matters of trade.

Our non-communist friends, by contrast, start with the premise that every great power aspires to enlarge its sphere of influence and to gain all the economic and strategic advantages it can, by peaceful means if possible, by war only if all other methods fail. They were deeply shocked, but not altogether surprised, when nazi Germany gambled on domination of Europe and Japan gambled on domination of Asia. They deplored the conduct of the Nazis and Japanese but did not detect a demonic aspect in the misdeeds of these twentieth-century conquerors that, aside from the technological changes in the arts of war, would set them wholly apart from Genghis Khan, Alexander the Great, Napoleon, or Kaiser Wilhelm II. Nor did the fact that fanatical Nazis and suicide-bent Japanese kamikazes acted with semireligious ideological fury make them seem so strange as to place them outside the pale of human experience. For non-communist nations recalled from their own histories the ideological ruthlessness of the Moslems and of the Spanish Inquisition, not to speak of lesser butcheries committed throughout the ages, frequently in the name of the Deity. This does not mean that they excused the Germans and Japanese — actually they have been far more slow than we in forgetting the cruelties of our wartime enemies and less sanguine about their reformation — but they looked on their actions with a greater sense of historical perspective.

In this perspective, too, the non-communist nations have viewed Russia, whose history under the Czars has in many instances been linked with their own. Russia's interest in the Baltic and the Dardanelles, in the North-West frontier of India and in Afghanistan, in Iran and Manchuria, was not so novel to the British and the Scandinavians, the Turks and the Indians, the Chinese and the Koreans, as it was to Americans, who in two centuries of national existence had had few direct contacts with the Russian Empire. Having frequently collided with Russia's territorial aspirations in the nineteenth century and the first decade of the twentieth, Britain was prepared to make a new series of arrangements resulting from the alterations in the balance of power produced by World War II. To give the most striking known example, Winston Churchill, who by no stretch of the imagination could be classified as either pro-Russian or pro-Communist and who has amply proved his friendship for the United States, saw nothing unreasonable or immoral in June 1944, six months before Yalta, in offering to divide with Russia, for military purposes, spheres of influence in Rumania, Hungary, Bulgaria, Yugoslavia, and

Greece. This offer, when made known in Washington at the suggestion of the Russians, provoked a profound moral revulsion on the part of Secretary of State Cordell Hull, who declared that the United States did not believe in such arrangements. The scheme, however, was finally approved on a temporary basis by President Franklin D. Roosevelt, after Churchill, when queried about the propriety of spheres of influence, retorted that the United States had a sphere of its own in Latin America.

Those Americans who have criticized the territorial and political arrangements made by the United States and Britain with Russia at the Yalta conference in February 1945 are certainly right, on moral grounds, in contending that the Western powers should not have left the fate of the nations of Eastern Europe in the hands of Russia and should not have acquiesced in proposed arrangements between the Kremlin and Chiang Kai-shek that ultimately proved detrimental to China. But quite aside from the consideration that the Yalta agreement was made at a time when the outcome of the war was still highly uncertain both in Europe, after the Battle of the Bulge, and in Asia, and the Western nations feared to lose Russia's support, the reality of 1945, which hindsight commentators are apt to forget, is that the United States and Britain were not in control of the situation in Eastern Europe, which had never been within their orbit, and had done practically nothing to assist the countries of that area when they became victims of German aggression in 1939. Nor did the United States, which had given extensive military and financial aid to Chiang during the war, find it possible to influence the domestic policies of the Generalissimo, who at that time was himself eager to arrive at a settlement with Moscow.

We have every right, on moral grounds, to denounce Russia's encroachments on the territories of neighboring countries and to resist these encroachments to the best of our ability. But if we are to convince other peoples of our reliability, it is essential that we should implement our moral principles with concrete actions — not only when aggression threatens, but in the daily give and take of world affairs. We must recognize that the rights of small nations, which today are menaced by communist Russia, have been under threat again and again throughout history. This has been true of Poland, divided by Russia, Germany, and, before 1919, Austria-Hungary; of Iran, buffeted between Britain and Russia; of Albania, caught in a tug of war between Italy and Yugoslavia; and so on. We, and the British before us (let us recall Lord Byron's poetic death at Missolonghi in a war to liberate the Greeks), have thrown ourselves with passion into struggles to help small nations cast off the yoke of great powers, without taking much time to consider whether these nations, once liberated, would find it possible to maintain their political and economic independence in an intensely competitive and danger-ridden world. The older great powers had long ago recognized this problem, and had taken care of it by methods which are unpalatable to us: by dividing the territories of small nations among themselves, as in the case of the four Polish partitions; or by staking out spheres of influence, as Britain and Russia did in Iran in 1907; or by bartering one small country or region for a free hand in another country or region, as Russia did in 1910 when she recognized Japan's control in Korea in exchange for Tokyo's recognition of Russia's special rights in Mongolia and Manchuria; or by incorporating them boldly into their territories, as Russia did with the Baltic countries in 1940, thereby preventing their impending seizure by Hitler.

None of these methods, and from the moral point of view quite rightly, has been sanctioned by the United States. Yet if the rough-and-ready ways of old-fashioned diplomacy are to be discarded, then new ways of protecting the rights and interests of small nations must be discovered. For many small countries, wedged in between powerful neighbors — such as Finland between Germany and Russia — the choice has often narrowed down to being conquered by one or another of the great powers or playing off one against another or, preferably, against a third in a precarious and usually perilous attempt to preserve at least a semblance of independence. The most promising way at present appears to be the possibility of placing disputed defenseless territories, for a time at least, under the guardianship of the United Nations to protect them as much as feasible against encroachments by all great powers. This is the procedure which has been suggested for Korea, if and when a truce is concluded and the country is unified. It is also the procedure favored by a number of UN members for the island of Formosa, a bone of contention in the United States not only because of its strategic position but even more because it is the refuge of Chiang Kai-shek. When we speak about the "liberation" of nations now under the control of the U.S.S.R., it is important that we should be ready to give these nations firm safeguards for the future against renewed encroachments not only by Moscow, but also by a reunited and rearmed Germany, which in the past has proved no more sensitive than Russia to the rights of small nations. Moral adjurations about freedom will not save the Poles and Czechs from another Munich.

Fortunately for us, the United States is not under the compulsions which have led other great powers in the past to seek new territories — the compulsions of lack of raw materials or food, the need for population outlets, the fear of attack by hostile neighbors. But with the development of air communications and the discovery of the atomic and perhaps now the hydrogen bomb, the United States is no longer in the favorable security position once guaranteed by its frontage on two oceans, with relatively weak and nonmilitant neighbors on its northern and southern borders. While this is not always acknowledged by Americans, who are convinced we have not extended our frontiers since World War II, the United States has in fact expanded all over the globe. Not only did it acquire by occupation, and subsequently by peace treaties and other agreements, the right to maintain armed forces in such advanced outposts as West Germany and Japan, traditional enemies of Russia, but it has built bases encircling Russia, from Morocco to Tripoli, from Britain to Saudi Arabia, from Greenland to the Azores. All these operations can be, and have been, justified by American spokesmen as merely a response to Russia's aggressive tactics, and are regarded here as solely defensive in character. Every great power, however, has always declared that its military preparations had defense alone as an aim, and has consistently denied all aggressive purposes, always attributing such purposes to its opponent. The United States, therefore, must be prepared to answer doubts on this score voiced not only by Russian and communist propagandists, but also by non-Communists in countries friendly to us who fear that defense might all too easily turn to offense, and that Washington, in a moment of nervousness, might carry its allies into a major war without consulting them.

Our non-communist friends, like ourselves, recognize that the U.S.S.R. is not only bent on expansion through political and economic controls over neighboring countries but also seeks ideological world domination through the activities of Communist parties in other countries. Where they have differed from us on many occasions in the past is in rejecting our concept of the struggle between unmitigated good and unmitigated evil. They do not believe that all the troubles and anxieties of the twentieth century are due to the machinations of the Kremlin and of native Communists. We often say that we are living in a revolutionary period, but do not always inquire into the reasons why the world is in revolution. Our friends are just as aware as we are that the Russians and the

Communists take advantage of all existing maladjustments, but they believe that these maladjustments were in the making long before 1917, and that even if Karl Marx had never written *Das Kapital* and Lenin had never established the Third International in Moscow, Europe and Asia, the Middle East, Africa, and Latin America would still be gripped today by far-reaching political, economic, and social problems. Just as our non-communist friends did not share our glowing hope that the victory of World War II could transform Germans and Japanese overnight into genuine practitioners of democracy, so they do not believe today that the disappearance of the Soviet government or the suppression of communist thought and the liquidation of Communist parties outside Russia would solve the problems besetting our age.

It is not a denial of the threat represented by Russia and communism to recognize the grave difficulties, created neither by Russia nor communism, with which the world would in any case have been confronted in the twentieth century. Among these difficulties, which have been aggravated by two world wars and unquestionably compounded by Russia and by native Communists, are the determination of peoples in colonial areas to achieve independence from the Western powers; the vast disparity in productivity between the nonindustrialized nations of Asia, the Middle East, and Africa, on the one hand, and the Western sector, on the other, and to a lesser extent also between Western Europe and the United States; the desire of the underdeveloped nations to retain for their own uses the raw materials they once furnished the Western industrialized nations in return for manufactured goods; the disintegrating effect of Western education, of industrialization, of technical achievements, on the social fabric of nonindustrialized nations; the reluctance of ruling groups in many countries to launch reforms; the disillusionment and frustration created even in the advanced nations by the wars, economic crises, and moral conflicts of our times; and the prevailing feeling that somehow or other, with the technological means placed at our disposal by modern science, human beings should be able to create something better than a world where too large a sector is still impoverished, fear-haunted, disease-ridden, and dominated by anxiety about another destructive war.

Even if Russia did not exist, we would still face two great enemies — poverty and nationalism. Poverty, if bereft of hope, leaves the masses of the population, even in the advanced Western industrial nations, exposed to the propaganda not only of the Communists, who appeal mostly to workers, peasants, and some intellectuals, but also of the Fascists and Nazis, who appeal to war veterans, small-business men, white-collar workers, and university students. In the opinion of our noncommunist friends, any program against Russia and communism which puts so much stress on the creation of armies and the manufacture of weapons as to reduce the still modest amount of consumer goods available at prices which the average man and woman in Europe — let alone in other continents — can pay is doomed to failure and could, in fact, deliver Europe to the Communists without the appearance of a single Russian soldier west of Berlin and the firing of a single shot. While our friends agree with us on the necessity of producing military strength sufficient to hold Russia at bay in case it should contemplate armed aggression, they are less hopeful than we about the efficacy of arms. They fear that once the military machine gets under way, it will be difficult to resist the temptation of allocating more and more of the world's skilled manpower and scarce raw materials to arms production, leaving civilian consumers to face an increasingly bleak standard of living with little hope of improvement for the future.

The United States, too, recognizes that the root of postwar

unrest is poverty, with communism the symptom rather than the sole cause of the disease. We made this clear by launching in 1947 the Marshall Plan, which was explicitly designed to combat in Europe the misery left in the wake of two world wars. Most Americans who supported the Marshall Plan, however, believed at first that the expenditure of American funds for the economic reconstruction of Europe would of itself create conditions favorable to democracy and thus reduce, if it did not altogether eliminate, the danger of communism. What they did not then foresee, and what many still do not understand, is that our financial and technical aid, without which Europe would have found it hard to make a rapid recovery, often did not directly benefit the workers and peasants who still see little improvement in their precarious living conditions.

Americans, who had hoped that economic aid would provide a genuine remedy against communism, were disappointed to discover in 1951 that the French national elections showed only a 2 per cent decline in the popular vote cast for the Communists, while the municipal and regional elections in Italy actually revealed a 6 per cent increase in the communist vote. It has been hard for us to understand that in Europe there is a marked distinction between what a contributor to *The Commonweal* calls "political communism" — that is, convinced adherence to the Communist party — and "social communism." "Social communism" represents a deep-seated distress on the part of millions of people who feel neglected by their governments and unable to achieve their modest objectives, and who turn to communism more as an expression of dissatisfaction with existing conditions than as an indication of ideological preferences.

In the underdeveloped countries of Asia and the Middle East, of Latin America and, more recently, North Africa, nationalism, reinforcing the demand for the eradication of poverty, has proved potentially as explosive a force as communism, and has often been equally hostile to the Western nations. It has been easy for landowners and feudal rulers of nations in these areas to turn away the wrath that impoverished peasants might otherwise have wreaked upon them by pointing to the misdeeds, real or fancied, of Britain, France, and more recently the United States. When nationalism has been fused with fanatical religious movements, as in Iran and Egypt, it has escaped the control even of those who first tried to utilize it for their own ends, and the Communists have capitalized on national sentiment to spur internal revolts as well as opposition to foreign "capitalists." Economic improvement might ultimately alleviate the tensions created by nationalism, and this we have recognized by launching a modest Point Four program of technical assistance to underdeveloped nations. But before the West can give effective economic assistance it has to overcome the suspicions and resistances evoked by memories of former colonial rule and of special economic and strategic advantages which it has hitherto enjoyed, from Iran and Indonesia to the Suez Canal and Bolivia. It is unrealistic for us to assume that unrest and dictatorship in the underdeveloped areas are inspired solely by communism. How then can we explain Mossadegh and Perón, President Ibáñez in Chile, and General Naguib in Egypt?

Our non-communist friends, aware of the explosive force of poverty and nationalism, find it difficult to understand the assumption made by many Americans that the communist seizure of power in China was due to the actions or failures to act of a few Americans who "sold China down the river." In their opinion it is extraordinarily brash for Americans to assume that intervention by this country would have altered the course of events in an ancient nation with a population of 400 millions, whose social, political, and economic fabric had been disintegrating for many years under the impact of West-

ern influence, Japanese conquest, internal discontent and dis-
sension, and reluctance on the part of the ruling group to
heed the people's desire for change, which the Communists
channeled into a far-reaching revolution. Once this revolution
did take place, the United States, rigidly maintaining the assumption that China had succumbed to the influence of Russia, although it had previously acknowledged the part played
by Chiang Kai-shek in the events that led to Communist victory, decided not to recognize the Peiping regime and then,
following the entrance of the Chinese Communists into the
Korean war, took the position, understandably, that it could
not grant recognition to an aggressor or permit its admission
into the United Nations.

Looking to the future, it will be necessary for the United
States, if it seeks the "liberation" of peoples subjugated or influenced by Russia, to decide what kind of political, economic,
and social order it will recognize in the liberated countries. It
is clearly impossible for the United States to sit on the lid
of revolutionary movements, like a twentieth-century Metternich, in the hope of thereby preventing an explosion that
might redound to the benefit of Russia. We could hardly urge
the liberated nations to accept anew the rule of groups like the
Iron Guard of Rumania or the Arrowcross of Hungary who
in the interwar period opposed reforms, and, if liberation were
achieved, would like to count on the United States to help
them check any future stirring of what they call "radicalism."
If we did this, the United States would become a sitting duck
for attacks by communist propaganda. For the Communists,
with some semblance of verisimilitude, could then assert that
America opposes not merely communism, but all attempts at
change, and even puts arms into the hands of those who in the
past have suppressed efforts at reform.

One of our problems is that the United States, except in the
case of Yugoslavia, has until now been reluctant to draw

a distinction between Russia and communism — between imperialist aggression by the Russian nation, which all countries menaced by the U.S.S.R. would want to resist, and communism as a doctrine in which many non-Americans who reject Russian's dictatorship fervently believe. Because of our profound repugnance for communism in general, and communist Russia in particular, we have found it impossible to separate the good from the evil, to draw a distinction between the brutalities of the police state ruled by a party dictatorship and the possibly valid achievements of the Communists in industrializing and modernizing underdeveloped areas, vast as the cost of these achievements has been in terms of human suffering and waste of materials.

Our tendency to condemn indiscriminately all that has happened in Russia or has been advocated by non-Russian Communist parties has placed us in a difficult position. Until recently the Communists, by urging land reform, more education for the masses, industrialization, independence from colonial rule, and other measures which we ourselves support, had seized the initiative in promoting change throughout the world. Yet in the final count the outcome of the struggle between democracy and communism will be determined by the capacity of each system to understand the world-wide desire for change and to satisfy this desire. The American people, who have shown a peculiar talent for adapting rapidly to new conditions, are in a far stronger position than the Russians, who are still far behind us, to assume the leadership in a revolution-minded world. In doing so, however, we must not rigidly insist that communist ideas and practices, which as we see in the case of Yugoslavia may appeal to other peoples, be discarded, but instead urge that these be shorn of political repression. An inescapable reality of our times is that change of all kinds must take place if we are to avoid further explosions. The question is whether the non-communist sector of the world has the imagination and courage to carry out change by democratic means, without resort to force, as contrasted with the violent coercive methods of communism.

Sooner or later the United States will have to rethink its attitude toward communism as distinguished from Russia. Our task in this respect is greatly complicated by the vast difference between the way in which we and our friends in Europe view the Communists. In this country it has proved impossible to believe that any genuine, normal, right-thinking American could possibly support communist doctrines, and it is assumed that all American Communists are either foreign-born, abnormal, or mentally unsound — an assumption which the rank and file of the numerically small American Communist party have done little to disprove. On the ground that all Communists are committed to overthrow the government by force and violence, the United States has taken stern measures to remove them from the political scene by prosecuting and imprisoning the party's leaders, although it has not gone on to the logical conclusion of outlawing the Communist party. While with half their minds Americans think of Communists as dangerous criminals and traitors, with the other half they are apt to think of them as creatures out of this world, something in the category of "The Thing," who have no relevance to American life as we know it.

However heinous the objectives and reprehensible the methods of European Communists, it is difficult to see how France or Italy could follow the example of the United States. For this would mean that they would have to silence several million people who at present vote Communist, expel and jail legally elected deputies from each of the national parliaments, not to speak of other legislative bodies, and expunge from men's minds ideas that, under existing conditions of poverty and lack of reforms, have acquired strong influence among noted and, in many cases, useful citizens.

Continuing opposition to communism here has also confronted the United States with difficult decisions as to the policy it should follow toward Marshal Tito, who has defied Stalin and his attempts at domination of Yugoslavia, yet proclaims himself a simon-pure follower of Marxism and Leninism — more pure than Stalin, in fact, because his communist faith is unadulterated by Russian deviations. In the case of Yugoslavia considerations of military and diplomatic strategy have prevailed over ideological differences. The possibility of detaching Belgrade from Moscow, of adding its hardy army, estimated at 32 divisions, to the as yet meager forces of the non-communist nations of Europe, and of thereby strengthening the Western outposts in Greece, Turkey, and the eastern Mediterranean, was thought sufficient to justify first economic, then military, aid to Yugoslavia in 1950–1952. Marshal Tito, for his part, undertook various changes in the political and economic institutions of Yugoslavia, with the announced purpose of making communism less bureaucratic and more humane — although his opponents still charge that Yugoslavia, in spite of such changes, remains a police state.

At the other end of the political spectrum a similar problem arose with respect to Franco Spain, whose dictatorial regime, unresponsive to demands for reforms on the part of businessmen and workers, of generals and clergy, of monarchists and even of elements in the Falange party controlled by General Franco, had aroused a great deal of opposition in the United States, and even more in Britain and France. Here again considerations of strategy, particularly the desire of some American military leaders to assure the defense of Western Europe by including Spain in the Western coalition, or at least by keeping it outside the Russian orbit, led the United States to soft-pedal its previously proclaimed opposition to fascism and, in the summer of 1951, to explore the possibility of linking Spain in some way to the North Atlantic defense system. Encouraged by the prospect of this development, Franco's associates made it known that the dictator was contemplating various reforms, among them the grant of more independent action to the members of the Cortes, the parliament of Spain. Thus in practice, although not yet in so many words, the United States has departed from the demonic theory of history, which attributed peculiarly evil purposes to fascism and communism, and has indicated its willingness to deal with countries dominated by the two abhorred systems, provided this seemed beneficial to American interests.

Ultimate judgment about this country's attitude toward the realities of world affairs will be based on the estimates that our friends, as well as nations still undecided about the side they should choose, will make concerning our objectives. Is the United States different from other great powers of the past? Will it be animated solely by disinterested motives of helping other nations, or will it pursue its own interests under cover of concern for the interests of others? Can it, unlike other great powers, succeed in building armaments without yielding to the temptation of using them in a war that would be described by us as defensive but that might be regarded by others as preventive? Will it forbear from the even greater temptation of using its unmatched capacity to make or break the economies of other nations in order to force them into accepting political, economic, and social institutions they may not want and that may not be suited to their needs?

It is important to bear in mind that the core of Yugoslavia's rebellion against Moscow was not a quarrel over ideological concepts, but profound disillusionment at the discovery that a "socialist" great power, which had been expected to show disinterestedness about small neighbors of like faith that would distinguish it from the predatory "imperialist capitalist" countries, turned out not to be above political domination and economic exploitation. Can the United States treat small nations with more sympathy and respect than other great powers have done in the past and thus acquire a position of leadership based not on military force or economic pressure, but on the moral principles we vigorously proclaim?

The answer to these questions cannot be given, in the first instance, in terms of foreign policy. Foreign policy is but a reflection of a nation's philosophy of life. Domestic and foreign policies are but two faces of the same coin. It is impossible to oppose change at home and press for it abroad; to carry the torch for anti-colonialism in Asia, Africa, and the Middle East, yet tolerate racial discrimination within one's own borders; to hedge the country with high tariff and immigration barriers, yet urge other nations to create free economic unions and to offer refuge generously to homeless people; to oppose feudalism in theory, yet help to perpetuate it in practice by economic and military aid to feudal governments.

The feeling of frustration, the indecision, the anxiety which we have experienced about our role in world affairs stem in large part from our inability, so far, to translate our basic national beliefs fully and unequivocally into terms of foreign policy. If we are to do so in the future we must first look inwardly upon ourselves, and rediscover the ingredients of our success at home so that we can inject these ingredients more vigorously into our foreign policy.

2

"AMERICA IS A HELL OF A SUCCESS"

D URING the century and a half when the United States was primarily absorbed in its own affairs and felt little or no responsibility for developments in other continents, Americans had no strong urge to explain their way of life or interpret their ideas to other peoples. True, some American tourists acting as "innocents" abroad, were known to boast about this country's achievements and to draw comparisons, not always flattering to our European friends, between the Old World and the New. Others, however, sought inspiration in the literature, music, art, scientific achievements, and legal institutions of Europe, and some found satisfaction in the life of expatriates in London, Paris, or Rome.

But until Western democracy and free enterprise had been challenged first by nazism and fascism in the 1930s and then, after World War II, by communism, we felt no necessity to convince other nations that the United States has achieved a society superior to that engineered by Hitler, Mussolini, or Stalin and has far more to offer to the nations of the world than do totalitarian dictatorships. We took this for granted and assumed others did likewise. Now, needled by various forms of criticism, we have come to the conclusion that we must tell our own story abroad, both to counteract misinformation spread by our opponents and to provide an accurate picture of the United States as we see it.

Propaganda — the propagation of ideas — is not new. It has been used for centuries both by churches and by secular states to sway men's minds and bend opinion this way or that in the direction desired. What is new today is the world-wide attempt to use propaganda as a substitute for military force by transforming it from a presentation of ideas into a battle of words dramatically described as psychological warfare.

As a result, the propagation of ideas, which conceivably could be carried on with a scrupulous regard for accuracy, is now often confused with strategically designed efforts to hit the opponent in a vulnerable spot. Straightforward description thus becomes merged, sometimes imperceptibly, with governmental debate. News is presented at selected moments not so much to report the true situation or aims of the country engaged in psychological warfare as to cause the maximum of embarrassment or harm to the opposite side. The oversimplification characteristic of modern mass media of communication — newspapers, radio, television — makes it more difficult, even with the best of intentions, to offer the qualifications which might temper the predisposition of psychological warriors to have the "pot call the kettle black." While much is said about the need to appeal to the minds of men, modern propaganda, as Professor H. A. R. Gibb, distinguished Britain Orientalist, has pointed out, is addressed chiefly to the emotions, and to the most primitive emotions at that, such as hysterical fear of communism, violent racialism, and the obscure passions latent in all human beings which rise frighteningly to the surface in periods of crisis. Nations long subjected to this psychological bombardment lose the capacity to question or criticize, and eventually even to reason. After being summoned day after day to distrust the opposing side, they reach the point where even the most reasonable action of the opponent becomes suspect, and his failure to act in a threatening manner arouses more anxiety than his actual resort to force. What is worse, the governments engaged in propaganda become so fascinated by their own operations and so enmeshed in them that they can no longer distinguish true facts and ideas from their own plans for battles of words, and they fall prey to what Professor Gibb calls "institutional delusion."

Today the United States is trying, at one and the same time, to tell a factual story and to fight a psychological war with the U.S.S.R. by methods ranging from verbal attacks to promotion of subversive activities which, in American opinion, are fully justified by the subversive activities conducted by the Kremlin in other countries. Can the two operations be successfully combined? Or may our battle to meet the challenge of communist ideas with ideas of our own be jeopardized and distorted by becoming mixed up with our battle of words to defeat, weaken, and subvert the Soviet government? Will our verbal attacks and counterattacks on communist propagandists leave us in the negative position of answering their strictures on our institutions, while we should be concentrating on the positive task of giving the rest of the world a true picture of our society? Does our propaganda enlighten those to whom we are addressing ourselves? Or do our words, when designed to achieve verbal victories over the Kremlin, merely confuse our friends, actual and potential, and widen the gap between us and the Russians? Is the voice of America making itself not only heard, but also understood, around the globe?

Our chief difficulty, as is natural in a democracy, is that America speaks not with one voice, but with many often contradictory voices. The people to whom we address ourselves are well aware that we are *against* Russia and communism. But what, they ask, are the majority of Americans *for?* If we answer in chorus that we are for democracy and free enterprise, they then bombard us with questions such as these:

"Then what about your support of Franco, of German industrialists who once backed Hitler, of Chiang Kai-shek, of
Marshal Tito, of Emperor Bao Dai in Indo-China? Why do
you speak of the Latin American countries as democracies
when you know that most of them are ruled by dictatorships?
Why do you object to socialism in Europe and Asia, yet insist that backward economies should be modernized through
far-reaching changes? Are you sure that you have a completely
free enterprise system at home as some of your prominent
spokesmen assert, or have you accepted a number of measures
which in one way or another limit free enterprise? Are not
some of these measures comparable to those you criticize in
Britain, New Zealand, Australia, and the Scandinavian countries? Is it true, as your propaganda says, that all difficulties in
nations like Iran and Indo-China are due primarily to Russia
and communism?" In short, the emphasis placed by American
propaganda on anti-communism often causes us to lose sight of
the fact that nations opposed to Russia's imperialism, whether
they are non-Communist, like Britain and Canada, or Communist like Yugoslavia, want to hear not only denunciations of
Moscow but also positive statements of the ideas to which a
majority of the American people feel they are dedicated.

Propaganda cannot be conducted in a vacuum. The most
elaborate and effective machinery for the transmission of broad-
casts and the publication of pamphlets about the United States
cannot prove successful unless it has substance with which to
work. There is no use concealing the fact that we have been
divided among ourselves concerning the values of the American way of life which we believe to be worth preserving here
and fostering abroad. Some of us support, others excoriate, the
concept and practice of "the welfare state." Some of us denounce all social reforms as "creeping socialism," others feel
we still lag far behind the needs of our times, and call for more
changes. Some urge the extension of civil rights, others want

to hold them in abeyance or restrict them. Some want to expand our participation in world affairs, others would like to see the United States "go it alone."

This diversity of opinion, particularly in an era of violent world controversy, must be both expected and welcomed in a democracy. We cannot hope to achieve nor should we seek to attain here one hundred per cent agreement on internal affairs such as is enforced under totalitarian dictatorships. But if we continue to differ profoundly about fundamental political, economic, and social issues, we cannot expect other nations, which must judge us by our acts, not merely by our words, to see us steadily and see us whole. If the men and women charged with the conduct of our propaganda abroad are to do an effective job, we must give them at least a general idea not only of what a majority of Americans are *against*, but also of what they are *for*.

Americans, not unlike other peoples, find it difficult to believe that there is anything wrong with them, and they are at a loss to understand why Indians or Britishers, Russians or Argentines, do not always entirely agree with this estimate. If there is one single characteristic which distinguishes us from other nations it is a buoyant optimism. This optimism has been encouraged and justified by the entire history of the American Republic, from the successful revolution against British colonial rule, through the exhilarating development of a largely uninhabited continent blessed with a remarkable combination of natural resources, to the command of a matchlessly secure geographic position.

This seemingly unending series of fortunate circumstances, so unlike the storm and stress suffered by other peoples, has understandably caused Americans to feel that anything is possible — that no situation is so difficult or perilous as to defy the American genius for overcoming all obstacles. No matter what qualms we may feel about this or that error or injustice in our society, this or that discrepancy between proclaimed ideals and actual practice, the vast majority of Americans remain ready to endorse the dictum of Speaker of the House, Joe Cannon, at the turn of the century that "America is a hell of a success."

What are the ingredients of this success? What are the aspects of our way of life of which we are particularly proud and which noticeably differentiate us from other people? What is the quintessence of our national qualities which we would most want to express in our foreign policy? To these questions different individuals are bound to give different answers. There are, however, six main features which immediately come to mind whenever we or our friends abroad pause to appraise the United States.

First, this nation, built from scratch by immigrants and descendants of immigrants, started out with a priceless advantage possessed by no other great power in history. It started free of the heritage of ancient prejudices and sharp social distinctions grown rigid through long acceptance, and free also of the territorial conflicts that have embittered life on the European continent and, to a lesser extent, in Latin America. In a new society, except for the preconceptions brought here by successive waves of immigrants, there was an initial inclination to regard every man and woman as being as good as any other — if not better. Every citizen began life with the assurance that, if he worked hard enough and had enough skill and talent, he could rise to the very top in whatever task he undertook — whether president of the United States or head of a great industry, whether distinguished musician or brilliant scientist. The sky was the limit; or, to use Napoleon's phrase about his army, "all careers were open to talent."

This social mobility, until recently in marked contrast to the social stratification of other countries, has encouraged and justified the prevailing belief that "nothing is impossible." In tackling any new task, an American, instead of first worrying about the difficulties it presents, promptly answers the question "Can this be done?" with a blithe "Why not?" or "Let's try anything once." The conviction that nothing is outside the range of the possible, that experimentation should never be deterred by precedents, is accurately reflected in the pragmatic philosophy of William James and John Dewey, a philosophy which is peculiarly American.

This faith in the experimental process, this willingness to devise new and still newer ways of doing things, are a natural result of the second outstanding feature of the United States — the heritage of its pioneering tradition. No other nation in modern history, except for Russia in Asia, has had the opportunity to open up virgin territory, to wrest land and resources from unexplored nature under physical circumstances that were a severe test of fortitude and determination. Instead of having to find an outlet for their energies in the exploration and development of overseas lands, often in climates ill-suited for white habitation, Americans were able to embark on overland colonization within boundaries they had staked out, with little opposition, as their own. Instead of building a great empire far from home on the precarious support of colonial peoples who were bound sooner or later to resent foreign rule, as the great powers of Western Europe did in Latin America, Asia, the Middle East, and Africa, Americans had the satisfaction of knowing that whatever land they acquired and developed would be either directly their own or at least part of their nation's undisputed domain. Thus they could build with confidence not only in themselves but in the future of their descendants. Pioneering was a vast national experiment, but an experiment with assured ultimate objectives. The confidence of the frontiersman, which is still an integral feature of the character of every American, was not that of an adventurer seeking a quick fortune. It was the confidence of a homesteader who felt he was laying the basis for a permanent structure, both personal and national.

The third outstanding feature of the United States, a direct result of the opportunity for pioneering in a new country, is the degree of liberty attainable here by the individual. The natural freedom of an unexplored, undeveloped land, combined with the rebellion against encroachments on personal freedom which brought pilgrims to our shores throughout this nation's history — from the signers of the Mayflower Compact to the displaced persons of our times fleeing totalitarianism in Europe — fostered here a deep-rooted belief in the necessity for recognizing and safeguarding free choice and activity in all spheres of life.

As this country evolved from a primarily agrarian economy into the greatest industrial power in history, the scope of the concept of freedom also profoundly changed. From the long-accepted freedoms of speech, religion, education, movement from one part of the country to the other as well as among different occupations, and organization of all kinds, we progressed to personal freedom for Negro slaves and, through the continuing expansion of political liberties to the increasing emphasis, in mid-twentieth century, on economic and social freedoms, to the four freedoms of Franklin D. Roosevelt.

Freedom of enterprise, initially unhampered by state intervention, brought many abuses which in the nineteenth century and early decades of the twentieth were denounced as acts of exploitation by "robber barons" at the expense of the small-business man and the consumer. But it also brought a vast expansion in productivity both in agriculture and in industry that ultimately, by making possible reductions in prices as well as increases in wages demanded by the labor unions, endowed this country with the highest standard of living known in history. The combination of rising productivity and social mobility created here a society which comes closer to being "class-less" than that of any other nation.

Viewing these developments in twentieth-century perspective, some American historians advocated at mid-century a revision of the criticisms hitherto made of the country's industrial giants. In their opinion the Rockefellers, the Carnegies, and others once denounced as "robber barons," by making possible this country's rapid industrial growth, had given it the strength to withstand the strains of two world wars and to survive the ideological crises of our times. By avoiding the pitfalls of monopoly, by expanding production instead of holding out for smaller output at higher prices as was done by many of the Western European producers, by recognizing the need to share the gains of industry with workers, consumers, and the community at large through philanthropic gifts, American capitalism escaped the paralysis which gripped European productivity in the later years of the Industrial Revolution. Thereby it defied the gloomy predictions of Karl Marx about the impending demise of capitalism.

This peaceful transformation, however, was made possible only because, after initial resistance to social adjustments, leading American industrialists recognized the need for accepting responsibility toward the community and for cooperating with the government, the labor unions, and the consumers in creating a more balanced and more stable economy. Now we must endeavor to make this spirit of cooperation sufficiently strong to permit the sacrifice of special interests by the various groups engaged in production — labor as well as employers, domestic manufacturers as well as exporters — which is required if the United States is to fulfill its far-flung commitments abroad without weakening its economy at home.

The struggle for freedom in the United States, as elsewhere, has not always progressed in a straight, unbroken line. There have been disillusionments and departures from avowed principles, notably in the treatment of our Negro fellow citizens. But these disillusionments and departures have sooner or later been publicly recognized, and sensitive Americans have experienced a feeling of guilt about failures on the part of this country to live up to its proclaimed ideals.

Since 1945 the strains and tensions of the cold war have precipitated a fresh controversy as to the meaning of freedom, and the extent to which citizens who criticize existing institutions and practices can be allowed to participate in political life, to teach, to make use of the media of mass communication. The controversy about the limits of personal freedom has focused particularly on the position of the Communist party in a democratic society. As internal tensions have risen, however, other questions have also been raised: such as whether critics of "free enterprise," even when they are not Communists, should be heard in a free-enterprise nation, or whether supporters of "progressive education" should be allowed to take a hand in the country's schools.

The struggle to arrive at a twentieth-century definition of liberty has been complicated by partisan name-calling and the introduction of the concept of "guilt by association," which seemed to contradict a basic American assumption that the individual is presumed to be innocent until he is proved guilty. Meanwhile, the significant influence of the Roman Catholic Church in the United States and President Truman's attempt to strengthen American cooperation with the Vatican in the fight against communism by the appointment of an ambassador to the Holy See, challenged the traditional separation of church and state and superimposed religious controversy on conflicts about competing ideologies and economic systems. In the midst of this reassessment of individual liberty, some Americans as well as many foreign observers asked whether the remarkable blossoming of freedom here had been due to deep-seated conviction or only to the accident of this country's unique history during which our institutions had seldom been seriously challenged at home or abroad.

The future of freedom in the United States is the most crucial issue at stake in the vast battle of democracy against totalitarianism. If this aspect of American life — the belief in the need to nurture and maintain the liberties of the individual — is allowed to decay, the United States, like Samson shorn of his mane, will be deprived of its most important source of strength in world affairs. With a record of freedom untarnished by fear-inspired restrictions, the United States can look forward with confidence to playing effectively its newly acquired role of world leadership. But let that record be placed in doubt, and this country will appear to other nations as just another great power using its armaments not for the defense of human liberties but for selfish interests of its own.

The emphasis on freedom has sometimes beclouded a fourth important aspect of American life: the significance of organized effort. Discussions of freedom here give the impression that Americans are concerned, first and foremost, with the rights of the individual and the protection of these rights against any encroachment or control by the state, which is regarded as something apart from and, on the whole, inimical to the individual. Yet one of the features of American society which particularly impresses non-Americans is the extent to which individuals are willing to subordinate their rights and interests, for the most part voluntarily, to various forms of cooperation with others, whether at the level of the local community, the state, or the nation, or in a wide range of professional and service groups. Americans, as seen from the outside, are the most highly organized people in the world. Here, again, the experience of pioneering days has had a lasting effect.

The vast complex of organizations that, like a telegraph network, covers this country has advantages as well as disadvantages. By cutting across racial, religious, professional, and political party lines that, in a new society, might otherwise have solidified into demarcations it would have later been hard to break down, our multifarious organizations offer a safeguard against undue influence and power by any one individual or group and help to cushion the shocks of adjustment by new citizens to the traditions and customs developed by the old. Organized effort has not only created here the most powerful modern machine for industrial and agricultural production, it has also fostered undertakings of all kinds, allowing ample room for education, for philanthropy, for opportunities of mutual aid which have given a feeling of hopefulness even to the least fortunate of our fellow citizens. These opportunities for community life have mitigated the disillusionment, insecurity, and frustration that in other nations fostered nazism, fascism, and communism.

There is, however, a reverse side to our predilection for organized activity. For this system, which maximizes the endeavors of the individual, at the same time tends to reduce the area in which the individual can operate according to his own peculiar interests or desires. Organized effort does not look kindly on the lone hand. The individual who does not seem to fit perfectly into the accepted groove may not be regarded as a complete misfit, or be ostracized, but he is apt to be viewed with latent suspicion as an eccentric or a nonconformist, if not as abnormal in some way. A paradoxical result of the existence in the United States, side by side, of a high degree of freedom and of highly integrated organization is that our society is less hospitable to persons of strongly individualistic bent than, for example, Britain or France, where departure from the ideas and practices accepted by the majority is regarded as a virtue rather than a defect, and nonconformism is not equated with subversion.

In a period of relative stability, the latent conflict between freedom and organization is concealed by a general sentiment of well-being and mutual respect or at least tolerance. In a period of crisis, such as we have been experiencing since 1945, the conflict bursts into the open. "The degree of tolerance attainable at any moment," said George Bernard Shaw in his preface to *Saint Joan*, "depends on the strain under which society is maintaining its cohesion." Once cohesion has been gravely strained, then, if the majority acts as an unthinking herd at the bid of a demagogic leader who appeals to its fears, the minority may be forced to remain silent if they want to survive. The most difficult problem we face at home today is how to discover and maintain that intangible line which separates organized effort from totalitarianism, and to permit, indeed encourage, the existence of nonconformist thought which fertilizes intellectual life and prepares the way for new advances in human relations.

Even in this critical period, however, the conflict between freedom and organization may be overcome by a gift which is the fifth important aspect of American life: the gift for compromise between seemingly irreconcilable points of view and of gradual evolution toward a middle course as contrasted with violent revolution. Not that the United States has been entirely free from internal strife. The Civil War, which entailed the loss of one million lives on the battlefield, was in effect a bloody revolution against conditions that peaceful means had failed to alter. But, on the whole, Americans have hitherto found it possible to meet around a table to discuss highly explosive issues and to adjust conflicts by peaceful methods of give-and-take instead of by resort to force, as has often happened in other countries.

It is significant that the American leaders who have received the highest and most lasting recognition have not been doctrinaire revolutionaries or intransigent military heroes but men who possessed the gift of compromise, who saw the need of conciliation and gradual change and who resisted the temptation to carry out decisions by coercion — George Washington and Thomas Jefferson, Abraham Lincoln and Franklin D. Roosevelt. Their ideas, which to many of their contemporaries appeared revolutionary, have become deeply imbedded in national thinking, and they remain alive today not as slogans to be quoted only on state occasions but as the actual working principles of the nation. The willingness to find a middle ground, the practical common sense — wary of all forms of extremism — which characterize Americans, these are in sharp contrast to the passions which again and again have swept other nations over the brink of catastrophe.

Not that Americans are free of prejudices and emotions which, under given circumstances, might result in dangerous explosions. In our generation we have witnessed the excesses of the Ku Klux Klan, the unbridled accusations of McCarthyism, and such displays of racial hatreds as the Cicero, Illinois, mob riots in 1951. But by and large there is still a deep-seated faith in this country that in any controversy, no matter how violent, reason can and must prevail, and earnest efforts continue to be made by thoughtful citizens of divergent points of view to find the common denominators on which a workable settlement might be based.

The dangers of overorganization have also so far been tempered in the United States by an unusually strong sense of personal responsibility for the improvement of the lot of human beings at home and abroad. This humanitarian impulse, the sixth significant feature of American society, has impressed even those non-Americans who are otherwise critical of the United States. Americans respond warmly and without second thought to the needs of suffering peoples, irrespective of race, creed, or political and economic ideology. While some of our foreign critics contend that our government-aid programs, such as the Marshall Plan and the Point Four program, are not wholly humanitarian in purpose but are designed to achieve clearly discernible political and military ends, this criticism can hardly be made of the generous contributions by Americans of all walks of life to a wide range of undertakings for the relief and education of people in other countries whom they have never seen and from whom they expect nothing tangible in return. No nation in history has given so much economic aid to other countries in time of peace as the United States, the amount of private and public contributions for foreign aid from 1945 to July 1, 1952 totaling 38 billion dollars. It can be argued, of course, that neither has any nation had so much to give, or been so fortunately spared the wars and war-produced disasters which have laid waste so many nations in this century. But other great powers also attained great wealth in their heyday, yet offered no comparable contribution to the common weal.

Americans, then, can justly feel that they have achieved "a hell of a success." This feeling has been well expressed by Henry Steele Commager in *The American Mind* * where he describes the thoughts of Americans in the nineteenth century:

"Nothing in all history had ever succeeded like America, and every American knew it. Nowhere else on the globe had nature been at once so rich and so generous, and her riches were available to all who had the enterprise to take them and the good fortune to be white. As nature and experience justified optimism, the American was incurably optimistic. Collectively, he had never known defeat, grinding poverty, oppression, and he thought these misfortunes peculiar to the Old World. Progress was not, to him, a philosophical idea but a commonplace of experience: he saw it daily in the transformation of wilderness into farm land, in the growth of villages into cities, in the steady rise of community and nation to wealth and power."

* Henry Steele Commager, *The American Mind* (Yale University Press, New Haven, 1951).

American optimism, the natural product of environment and historical circumstances not duplicated elsewhere on the globe except perhaps, on a lesser scale, in Russia, is a unique characteristic of this nation in modern times — although such diverse observers as Bertrand Russell and the French novelist Albert Camus believe that comparable faith in the future has been shown by the Russians. It would be interesting to discover whether the buoyancy and resiliency we have come to regard as commonplace in the United States are due to our material circumstances or are found in every nation in a given period of history — notably among the English from the Elizabethans to the Victorians, and among the French in the days of Louis XIV and Napoleon. Whether our seemingly unshakable belief in continued technological improvement and material well-being will be eroded by harsh experience, as it was in the case of the nations of Western Europe, or will triumph over all hardships, only the future can show.

Meanwhile we have carried our optimism from the sphere of domestic affairs, over which we had unchallenged control, into that of world affairs as the United States emerged from relative isolation. The zest aroused by decades of pioneering made Americans believe that on the world scene, too, nothing was impossible and everything should be tried at least once — a League of Nations, self-determination of peoples, integration of Europe, cooperation between ancient enemies like France and Germany, the democratization of the Germans and the Japanese, the termination of colonial rule, and the industrialization of underdeveloped areas.

It took us time to discover, often with a profound sense of shock as in the case of China, that we cannot hope to exercise the same control over the affairs of other nations that we can over our own — unless, of course, we choose to resort to force, which would automatically destroy our claim to democratic leadership. While we retained our national faith in the perfectibility of man — a faith which, paradoxically, is shared to-day only by fanatical Communists and which in older nations has been severely undermined by recurring wars, depressions, and revolutions — we gradually began to discern the limitations of possible action in other continents whose climatic, historic, political, and economic conditions vastly differ from our own. The atomic bomb, which we were the first to use and on which we relied as an ultimate deterrent to aggression against us, proved a boomerang: for it shook our confidence in the preservation of our national security without ultimately offering us protection from attack. Our dynamic desire to find a quick solution of a given problem so as to clear the way for the next task was sharply checked in many instances by the need to adjust our expectations and aspirations to the realities of life in other nations which we had somehow hoped to by-pass or to overcome by technical means. Our close-up view of the problems of many peoples whom we had barely known before 1945 tempered our natural buoyancy and caused us to reconsider the modern world and our relationship to it in a mood of soberness entirely new to Americans. To quote Professor Commager again:

"Although still persuaded that his was the best of all countries, the American of the mid-twentieth century was by no means so sure that his was the best of all times, and after he entered the atomic age he could not rid himself of the fear that his world might end not with a whimper but with a bang. His optimism, which persisted, was instinctive rather than rationalized, and he was no longer prepared to insist that the good fortune which he enjoyed, in a war-stricken world, was the reward of virtue rather than of mere geographical isolation. He knew that if there was indeed any such thing as progress it would continue to be illustrated by America, but he was less confident of the validity of the concept than at any previous time in his history."

This more mature evaluation of the world, this attempt, novel for us, to measure other nations not by the yardstick of our unique experience but in terms of their particular historical circumstances, has not, however, destroyed the conviction that the United States is the most successful country in the world and offers the most satisfying way of life ever achieved by human beings. Closer contacts with other peoples have only served to confirm this impression and to reinforce faith in our institutions, our way of life, and our destiny as the leading nation in the modern world. Nor has there been much predisposition to think that we should alter our society to meet the criticisms or fit the needs of other countries, although many Americans feel it quite proper to insist that our friends in Europe and Asia should effect political, economic, and social transformations according to patterns we regard as desirable. Instead, in 1951 some of our political leaders began to talk in terms of repudiating the United Nations in favor of a new form of isolation or of unilateral action unhampered by "entangling alliances." This trend, too, reflected confidence — confidence that the United States had sufficient strength and wisdom to weather alone the storms of our times, and that whatever test awaited us in peace or war would see this country the ultimate victor.

Granting that the United States is "a hell of a success" and may hope to remain so, many Americans assume that what seems obvious to us must be equally obvious to other people. It shocks and grieves them to discover that we are not always seen abroad in the roseate glow of our own estimation. When they hear that others do not automatically or uniformly like us, or are less sure than we of our good intentions, they feel divided between the impulse to "make" the rest of the world accept our image of the United States by expanding and perfecting propaganda about our way of life, and disdainful rejection of the judgment of our critics as irrelevant and inconsequential. "Why should we care what other people think of us?" it is often asked. "Our way is good enough for us — if they don't like us, let *them* go back where they came from!"

This conclusion may seem desirable, but it is becoming less and less practicable. The United States, whether we like it or not, must care about what others think of us. Much as we might prefer to have this country become a great power wholly independent of the likes or dislikes of actual or potential allies, the stark truth is that the United States would be gravely crippled, perhaps completely paralyzed, if in case of war with the U.S.S.R. it could not count on the sympathy and support of nations in other continents. Under conditions of modern warfare, the United States cannot afford to "go it alone."

Our best hope of keeping aggressors far from our shores is to base our military operations on the territories of other nations. Bases, however, will prove hollow defenses unless we gain active support of our policies by the peoples on whose soil they are constructed. Otherwise, we shall be in constant danger of being stabbed in the back. If we are to maintain cordial relations with the countries which permit us to share their territory for our common defense, we must endeavor to understand the psychology of their peoples and win them over to our view of the world by persuasion and not by the kind of coercion we denounce when it is employed by Hitler or Stalin. For us, understanding of other nations is no longer a pleasant academic exercise inspired by idealism. It has become a matter of life and death.

What, then, do other people think of us, and how can we correct seeming misconceptions on their part about our way of life and our objectives in world affairs?

3

WHAT'S WRONG WITH
THEIR FOCUS?

FROM our point of view, the United States, whatever its
faults and weaknesses, is a great democracy among whose
assets are enormous economic strength, actual and potential,
a progressive social system, and a dynamic, generous-minded,
forward-looking population highly skilled in the techniques
of modern industry and agriculture. Why, then, many Americans ask, don't other people see us that way? What's wrong
with *their* focus? Are they the victims of communist or other
propaganda which blinds them to America's true values? Are
they deluding themselves for some ulterior motive which for
the moment escapes us? Or, more disturbing thought, is it just
possible that they see some of our traits as they really are, not
as we fondly imagine them to be?

In trying to understand why other people think of us as
they do, it may be helpful to bear two things in mind. First,
no great power at the peak of its success is ever loved by smaller
and weaker nations, no matter how good its intentions may be.
This is an occupational hazard of great powers. Neither Rome
nor Greece, nor the France of Louis XIV and Napoleon, nor
the England of Queen Elizabeth and Queen Victoria, nor the
Russia of Alexander I, nor Germany under Kaiser Wilhelm
and Hitler, nor Austria-Hungary under Metternich, escaped

the onus attached to power. It would be unreasonable for the United States to expect that it will inspire greater affection on the part of other nations than its predecessors in world history. A great power may hope to be feared or respected. It cannot expect to be loved.

Second, it is untrue that other peoples "hate" us, as is sometimes asserted by overwrought American travelers. This may be disturbing to our national ego, but actually millions of human beings all over the globe have only a dim notion of America and Americans. If they do know something about us, it is usually through whatever shred of information happens to have swum within their ken — whether Abraham Lincoln or Hollywood, the American Revolution or fast automobiles, prodigious industrial production or chewing gum. Even in countries where communist propaganda, unopposed, has left no means untried to prove that the United States is a warmongering nation ruled by Wall Street moneybags who suck the blood of the poor, there is little evidence that the average man and woman — as distinguished from politicians, intellectual leaders, and others who have the opportunity or are under the necessity of formulating their thoughts about this country — have a feeling of hostility toward Americans. This is particularly striking in the case of Russia, where we have only scant possibilities of combating anti-American propaganda and yet where, according to the testimony of reliable observers, the Russian people remain both friendly and curious about the United States.

It would be a complete misrepresentation of the attitude of other nations toward us to assume that they do not see our good qualities or paint us solely in dark colors. A glance at the considerable literature about American life contributed by non-Americans since the birth of the United States shows that visitors to our shores agree with us in their estimate of our outstanding virtues. They describe us as the most progressive people in the world, the most hard-working, and as superb organizers. They admire our belief in progress, our profession of democracy, our sportsmanship, our social mobility, our spirit of service, our generosity toward each other and toward peoples of foreign lands. Above all, they are impressed by our faith in the future, by our unquenchable optimism. A Swedish commentator, Fredericka Bremer, said: "If you ask me what the people of the New World have got that the Old World lacks, then I would answer, warmer hearts, and a more energetic and youthful way of life." And another Swede, Victor Vinde, writing about America at war in 1942, concluded: "Consciously or unconsciously it is for this conception of life, slowly emerging from the undisciplined capitalism of the 'twenties and the depression and social experiments of the 'thirties that the American is fighting. He knows: there will be a tomorrow, he believes in tomorrow."

What, then, do other peoples *not* like about America? When we tabulate some of their dislikes, we find that their estimate of our faults is not very different from the estimate we make ourselves — with the usual human qualification that it is much easier to bear criticism from members of the family than from outsiders. The French writer Georges Duhamel, disgusted by a glimpse of the Chicago slaughterhouses, wrote between the wars: "I see men enough in America, but where are their souls?" Salvador de Madariaga, well-known Spanish interpreter of national characteristics, declared during the same period that "Americans are boys" who need new toys and gadgets, and who are afraid to be alone for fear that they might begin to think. Foreign observers have complained of the American passion for money-making. They have claimed that technique here is an end in itself, that life has become too mechanized in America, that we have overpowering standardization not only of things but of people which ultimately leads to conformity, precursor of totalitarianism, and that our desire for "the typi-

cally American" makes us fearful of "heretics," of all noncon-
formists. They have been struck by what they regard as our
"adolescence" (others have viewed this aspect of our lives as
heartening youthfulness), our lack of maturity as compared
with other nations.

Some, notably the French, have deplored our lack of per-
ceptiveness for culture — by which they usually mean cultural
values reserved in other lands for the elite. Others have felt,
with Madariaga, that our "combination of materialism with the
gregarious tendency" spelled the doom of our growth as a nation. Still others found much to criticize, before and during
the depression of the thirties, in our "irresponsible capitalism"
which a Chinese observer, No Yong-Park, described at that
time as "economic feudalism" comparable to the military feudalism of the Chinese warlords. Our attitude toward our Negro
fellow citizens has been one of the most outstanding and vulnerable targets for attack. And many foreign visitors have
been repelled by our chase for "the almighty dollar," our passion for advertising, and our predilection to act as "boosters."

Most of these criticisms have not, in the first instance, been
made by Communists or other avowed enemies of the United
States. Some of them have come from men and women who
felt deep admiration and affection for this country and hoped
that, with time, we would grow in stature, maturity, and influence. Nor should their comments surprise readers of our
own self-critics, of Thorstein Veblen and Sinclair Lewis, of
John Dos Passos and Upton Sinclair, of John Steinbeck, Lillian
Smith, and William Faulkner.

What we are confronted with, then, is not an impenetrable
barrage of hatred, but something far more difficult to penetrate:
and that is an accumulation of doubts, fears, and suspicions concerning our way of life, our motives, our ultimate aims. Nor
would it be accurate to say that this gamut of emotions is restricted to any national group, or to any social sector of a given

nation. It has become customary here to believe that only in Russia is the image of the United States subjected to distortion. Yet a careful study of the misinterpretations and outright untruths of Soviet propaganda made by Frederick Barghoorn, former American press attaché in Moscow, and reported in *The Soviet Image of the United States*,* shows that many similar misinterpretations are also found in Britain and Syria, in France and India, in Italy and Argentina.

Have we already forgotten that the Nazis before World War II, parroted today by the postwar neo-Nazis, described the United States as a "decadent democracy" — a situation Hitler attributed to the presence of Negroes and Jews in our midst? Is communist propaganda responsible for the fact that Stalin and Perón denounce American "capitalism" as a form of "imperialism"? What connection is there between the charges of Indian Socialists, French Gaullists, German neo-Nazis about the alleged attempts of the United States to dominate the world and deprive other nations of their sovereignty? How are we to explain a situation in which devout Catholics, fervent Communists, militant Moslems, and fatalistic Hindus agree in deploring American "materialism"? And how, to look at another side of the picture, are we to interpret the unanimity of some European industrialists and Asian feudal rulers in deprecating the "revolutionary" policies of the United States and hoping that "conservatism" may come to power in Washington? It would be a dangerous oversimplification to assume that Russia and the Communists alone depict us in a false light, and that if we could only silence the Kremlin's propaganda the United States would be able to bask in the sunshine of universal approval.

Nor should we delude ourselves into thinking that a conservative government abroad would be more likely to accept

* Frederick Barghoorn, *The Soviet Image of the United States* (Harcourt, Brace and Company, New York, 1950).

American policy unquestioningly than a government controlled by Socialists or Communists. Winston Churchill, the moment he returned to power in October 1951, promptly showed that he wanted to be a leader, not merely a follower, in the making of Anglo-American policy. The feudal authoritarians of the Middle East and the military dictators of Latin America have proved as defiant of the United States and, on occasion, as rabidly anti-American as Communists; and, by contrast, communist Marshal Tito of Yugoslavia has found it possible to conduct delicate negotiations with Washington in a conciliatory spirit. The circumstances of a given international situation rather than the ideology of the particular government with which we are dealing are apt to determine its attitude toward the United States.

It is also unrealistic to assume that only the "proletariat" of other nations, peculiarly vulnerable to communist propaganda and understandably envious and resentful of the riches of the United States, is our principal critic in world affairs. For while it is true that the Communists recruit the largest number of their followers among factory workers and poorer peasants, they still have in their ranks, or have had in the recent past, some of the most distinguished intellectuals of Europe, Asia, and Latin America — writers, scientists, painters, musicians, philosophers, teachers. In fact it is this intellectual elite, not the communist rank and file usually absorbed in the daily struggle for economic survival, who have expressed and propagated the most barbed criticisms of American ideas and practices. Nor is it yet clear that those among them who have repudiated the Communist party, like Arthur Koestler, have thereby found a spiritual haven in American democracy.

More perplexing for Americans is the critical attitude toward our way of life displayed by non-Communists — those elements of the middle class in Europe who, instead of espousing democratic ideals, drift into neo-nazi and neo-fascist movements, and those anti-Communists in Asia and elsewhere who, while fiercely opposing communism, themselves foster fanatical programs inspired by racial and/or religious dogmas. Still more alarming is the knowledge that some of the better-educated members of the young generation, well-favored by fortune, are known for their anti-Americanism, their fear of domination by the United States, their interest in communism, and their search to discover a "third" way of life which would eschew both Sovietism and Americanism. What might be understandable, if resented on the part of Aneurin Bevan, the erstwhile Welsh miner, or Frédéric Joliot-Curie, the French scientist, becomes baffling when discovered among men and women who seem "like us."

How can this be, we ask? How is it possible that other people, who either won their freedom in past centuries or aspire to win it today, can even think that the United States and the U.S.S.R. are comparable? What unhallowed influence can so distort their judgment and becloud their vision? How explain that the United States, which to us is the epitome of the best features of Western civilization, appears imperfect in so many respects to Europe and Asia, to the Middle East, Africa, and Latin America? What curious sea change does our system undergo that makes it lack abroad the appeal it has at home?

To a considerable extent, criticisms of the United States are based on sheer lack of information about the actual workings of our institutions. For example such otherwise well-informed people as the Scandinavians still know little about the broad program of social reforms, notably social security, unemployment insurance, and old-age pensions which has been developed in the United States during the past twenty years. Lack of information, however, is remediable. The information services of the United States, both public and private, can fill existing gaps by regularly providing accurate and simply presented facts about this country. But before we try to tell our story to other nations, it is important to discover what they think of us and why — and to decide, in all honesty, which of their judgments about the United States are based on misconceptions or actual falsehoods and which are justified criticisms that we may find it advisable and possible to correct.

Questions abroad concerning our way of life can generally be classified under five headings: (1) the strength of our democracy; (2) the degree of "materialism" in our culture; (3) our concept of modern economics; (4) our attitude toward colonialism; and (5) our concept of world politics.

Mere description of our institutions is not enough to dispel misapprehensions outside our borders. In an era of intensive propaganda from many sources, from Goebbels to Stalin, words once freighted with meaning have become demonetized through mechanical repetition or through overuse by governments representing widely different ideologies. Deeds will prove more persuasive than words in conveying the essence of the United States to other nations.

This is particularly true when we attempt to describe the content of our democracy, the day-to-day operation of American society as compared with Fourth of July orations. In trying to explain what we mean by democracy, we find it necessary to make sure that by our actions we do not disillusion other peoples, causing them to shrug their shoulders skeptically and to say: "What's the difference between the United States and the U.S.S.R.? A plague on both their houses!"

What are the aspects of our democracy which produce doubts abroad? Leaving aside familiar nagging comments about the lynching of Negroes, the principal question asked of us is: "To what extent does your democracy really safeguard the freedom you urge other people to practice?" Once this question has been raised, the conversation may take many twists and turns, depending on the interlocutor. "Is it not true that you discriminate against Negroes?" your friends from Asia,

Africa, and the Middle East will ask. "How can you reconcile this with your professions of democracy?" A Chinese or
a Filipino, wryly recalling our past aspersions on their alleged
political corruption, will inquire not without irony how we
explain the unsavory political links with the underworld revealed by the Kefauver committee or the "fixing" practices in
our favorite sports. Europeans and Asians alike find it difficult
to understand how the United States can reconcile the jail-
ing of Communists with the continued legal existence of the
Communist party or why it believes that communism will be
eliminated by imprisonment and deprivation of employment.
Few people abroad find character assassination, "guilt by association," the withholding of passports, loyalty oaths, gag rules
on speakers, or encroachments on academic freedom, com-
patible with the democratic ideals which we proudly proclaim
and advocate for other nations.

Thus the picture we paint, and in which most of us believe,
of an American democracy where freedoms flourish unrestricted and all inhabitants can say and do what they please
seems very different to our best friends abroad who see here,
instead, the spread of intolerance, the acceptance of some of
the racist ideas made odious by the Nazis, resort to repressions
dangerously reminiscent of the communist methods we profess
to abhor, and earnest efforts to achieve and enforce an American form of "thought control." Our friends abroad do not
believe the United States is doomed to follow the example of
nazi Germany. They are convinced that there are enough
healthy antibodies in our political system to combat the disease of totalitarianism. What disturbs them is to find how few
among us have been disturbed by the rapidly changing climate of opinion here, which alarms even conservatives in
Europe and Asia but leaves many Americans indifferent, partly
because they no longer notice the change. This apathy, in the
opinion of our foreign friends, is the most frightening symptom

of our current fear of communism. Our friends also wonder whether the democracy we have held up to the rest of the world as a shining example did not flourish here in the past largely because it had never been seriously challenged. Once the danger of even relatively limited opposition arises, they ask, will Americans silence or extirpate the challengers?

Closely linked to these questions about our democracy is the attitude of other nations toward what they call American "materialism." Here again is a word which has different interpretations depending on who uses it. Our friends as well as our foes contend that Americans are interested primarily not in spiritual and cultural values but in material gains — in earning a lot of money so that they can acquire as many material possessions as possible, such as houses, automobiles, vacuum cleaners, refrigerators, plumbing equipment, and gadgets of all kinds. We ourselves foster this impression by the advertisements picturing a householder's dreamworld which are carried in our large-circulation magazines, notably *Time* and *Life,* and which are seen by many abroad — advertisements that stress the desirability and even the sheer necessity of owning material possessions of all kinds or else suffering an intolerable sense of deprivation.

This impression is reinforced by the rich-looking, suave settings of many Hollywood films, which convey the belief to foreign audiences that most Americans live in the luxurious ease of urban penthouses and impressive country estates, with never a care about the sordid details of the daily grind, faced by the majority of human beings, of making both ends meet. Nor do we encourage other peoples to form a different concept of our civilization when we admit that more money is spent here annually on liquor and cosmetics than on books, paintings, music, and other nonmaterial objects. Only the relatively small numbers of foreigners who are able to come to the United States on extended visits can discover for themselves that most of our people, while infinitely better off than the rest of the world, live in relatively modest circumstances, and that large numbers of us do find satisfaction in intellectual and cultural pursuits.

To us it seems obvious that the impression abroad of the United States as a blatantly "materialistic" nation completely overlooks all the nonprofit, volunteer activities for the benefit of the community in which so many of us are engaged, and from which we receive no dividends except in terms of personal satisfaction. Nor does this impression of us take into sufficient account the generous desire of most Americans to aid, with no thought of material return, the helpless and hopeless of other lands. Bertrand Russell, who never hesitates to act as a friendly critic of the United States, has pointed out that "a great deal of nonsense is talked about American so-called 'materialism' and what its detractors call 'bathroom civilization.' " He does not think Americans are any more "materialistic" than other peoples. "A willingness to sacrifice income for idealistic reasons," he contends, "is at least as common in America as in England," and "the belief that Americans are fonder of money than we are is mainly inspired by envy." Writing in the same vein, Perry Miller, professor of American literature at Harvard University, says that the level of life in the United States "excites simultaneously both revulsion and envy," and that "all too often European criticism of America is a transparent effort to deny to the common man in Europe what he, transported to America, believes he has achieved or can achieve." *

We, for our part, are often inclined to speak critically of the "materialism" of other peoples — by this we mean such things as the alleged acquisitiveness and stinginess of the French, the desire of British workers for free teeth and spectacles, and

* Bertrand Russell, Perry Miller, and others, *The Impact of America on European Culture* (Beacon Press, Boston, 1951).

the eagerness of underdeveloped lands to obtain the mechanical prerequisites of modern industry and agriculture — without always realizing that for them, as for us, machinery and
money are means toward the end of improving their living
standards, not necessarily ends in themselves. Yet we often
assume that money is a panacea for the difficulties of poorer
countries, that a check or a financial appropriation can set-
tle almost any problem, and that Iran or Indonesia, not to
speak of Russia and China, might change their political course
if they only received a sufficiently large loan or grant from the
United States. This point of view was strikingly illustrated
during Iran's oil nationalization crisis in 1951, when it took
us a good deal of precious time to understand that the Iranians
would rather let their oil fields go to wrack and ruin than leave
the British-controlled Anglo-Iranian Company in command of
their single most important national resource; and that no
amount of American money would stop them from carrying
into effect a deeply felt conviction compounded of national
revolt against foreign intervention and passionate desire for
independence from all outside pressure, no matter how benevolent. What we discovered in Iran, and must bear in mind for
the future, is that what may seem like sordid "materialism" to
one nation represents legitimate national aspirations to another.

While it is untrue that Americans are solely preoccupied
with the acquisition of material goods, we often create the
impression abroad that our judgment of the ability of other
peoples is based primarily on their capacity to produce and to
purchase products which, in our opinion, would enhance their
living standards: bathtubs, radios, television sets, washing machines, and so on. It seldom occurs to us that the British or
Indians, Russians or French, might prefer to earn less money
and enjoy more leisure rather than work harder in response

to special financial incentives for the purpose of buying more things. For example, Anne O'Hare McCormick of *The New York Times* reports the surprise of a prominent American when he learned at a meeting with a group of Labor party back-benchers, that "they were not interested in the gadgets — refrigerators, vacuum cleaners, television sets, etc. — that typify the American standard of living." What they desire, he found, "is a well-organized Socialist state where the people live on a modest scale, with a thirty-five-hour work week, leisure and sports for all, and security in old age." Other Americans, for example the economist Harry Schwartz, deplore the low estate of Russia's economy, commenting on the fact that only in 1951 had Soviet industry started mass production of durable consumer goods such as washing machines, refrigerators, and television sets without inquiring whether even under more favorable circumstances Russians have the same eagerness to obtain these goods as Americans. In discussing the relative materialism of the United States and of other nations, it might help if other people would understand that we do not live by mechanical gadgets alone, and if we for our part would be willing to see that nonmaterial achievements may be more significant to other nations than the creation of industrial products.

A need for mutual readjustment of disputed concepts arises also with respect to our attitude toward the word "colonialism." Americans regard themselves as wholly different from the Western European nations which have had colonial empires in the past or still cling to remnants of these empires today: for we think of the United States as a traditionally anti-colonial country. It comes as a shock to us when we discover that the peoples of former colonial territories or areas still ruled by colonial powers often identify our policy with that of Britain, France, and the Netherlands in their

imperialistic prime. We find it difficult to see why the peoples
of Asia and the Middle East judge all Westerners, including
ourselves, by the experience they have had with Western imperialism over many decades.

   Yet whenever a crisis arises in underdeveloped areas which
appears to threaten the remnants of British or French domination, as in Iran, Egypt, Indo-China, or French Morocco,
and thereby to benefit Russia and communism, some Americans, even among the best-informed, react by saying that the
United States must take "strong action" to prevent anarchy
at strategic points, such as the Suez Canal, and to defend territories whose peoples "are not yet ready for self-government"
or whose governments "are incapable of providing adequate
defense." This reaction may seem entirely natural to us at a
time when national-security considerations overshadow our
former desire to promote the independence of colonial peoples.
But to the colonial peoples themselves it sounds like just another version of "the white man's burden," propounded by
the United States to justify its decision to take over the
heritage of empire which Britain is no longer financially able
to carry. "When therefore," says Professor F. S. C. Northrop
of Yale University, author of *The Meeting of East and West*,
"two world wars have depleted Great Britain's former strength
as the leading Western power and the United States has become in fact the most powerful Western nation, it becomes
easy for Middle Easterners and Asians to conclude that Western imperialism has merely shifted to the United States the
power through which it expressed itself. Nor do statements
by President Truman that the United States is in Korea merely
to prevent aggression and to permit Asians to run their affairs
in their own way suffice to alter this judgment. The Middle
Eastern and Asian peoples have been accustomed in the past
to Western imperialistic nations which have moral and political
arguments convincing to themselves for maintaining Western

troops and political administrators on Middle Eastern or Asiatic soil." *

Deplorable as the attitude of the peoples of the erstwhile colonial empires may seem to us, it would be wise to understand here that while anti-Western sentiment has been unquestionably sharpened and organized by the Communists since World War II, it antedated the propaganda of Lenin and Stalin and is by no means identical with communism. This sentiment, which is anti-foreign, not merely anti-Western, might easily turn against Russia as much as against the Atlantic nations if the Russians display in Asia the overbearing mien and the contempt for nonwhite peoples which in the past characterized many Western colonizers. It would persist even if the Kremlin were atomized tomorrow. The link between Russia and the underdeveloped areas of Asia and the Middle East is forged not so much by Communist ideology as by the deep-seated suspicion of all things Western which has existed among the Russians for centuries, sometimes in endemic form, sometimes bursting into sudden violent displays of xenophobia, from the days of Ivan the Terrible to the days of Stalin.

In Russia, as in other lands relatively untouched or not touched at all by the forces that have wrought Western civilization — Roman law, Latin Christianity, the Renaissance, the Reformation, the English, French, and American revolutions, the Industrial Revolution — a constant struggle has gone on between the infinitesimally small minority of educated people who admire the progress achieved by the West and want their nations to imitate it and the vast majority who either resent and envy this advanced development, or fear it, or want to have nothing to do with it on the ground that the Western way of life would spell the doom of local traditions and customs as well as religious beliefs which they hold precious. This view

* F. S. C. Northrop, "Asian Mentality and the United States Foreign Policy," *The Annals*, July 1951, pp. 118, 125.

of the West as both challenge and menace constitutes a common denominator between Russia, China, India, Japan, and other Asian peoples, and the Moslem world from North Africa to Pakistan.

The ruthless attempts of Russia's Czar Peter the Great in the early years of the eighteenth century to transplant Western methods of production and Western social manners to Russian soil; the vigorous polemic of the nineteenth century between the pro-Western writer Alexander Herzen, who spent many years in exile in England, and the pro-Slav critic Belinski; the bitter anti-Westernism of Dostoevski, prophet of Pan-Slavism; the clashes between the Westernized Trotzky and the anti-Western Stalin who has never been outside Russia (except to the Teheran and Potsdam conferences) — all these have parallels in India and Jordan, in China and Iran. While the pro-Western Prime Minister Jawaharlal Nehru advocates birth control for India, the pro-Hindu traditionalist, one-time president of his Congress party, Purushottamdas Tandon, rejects modern medicine as harmful to the ancient Hindu way of life. And even the modern-minded Nehru fails to carry through Parliament the bill which would modernize the position of women in India, and is denounced for his failure by the Columbia-trained leader of the Indian untouchables, B. K. Ambdekar. While King Abdullah of Jordan, a friend of the West, sought reconciliation of the Arabs with Israel, his opponents, one of whom assassinated him in July 1951, saw in Israel, with its modern outlook and its efforts to create an industrial society in an area of primitive agriculture, the embodiment of all the evils of Western civilization which, in their opinion, is inimical to Islam. Within Russia itself, in spite of the use of coercion by the Soviet government which, in many respects, has followed the policy of Peter the Great of "raising Russia on its hind legs," to quote the poet Alexander Pushkin, the Kremlin encountered stubborn opposition among its

Moslem citizens to such attempts at modernization as the un-
veiling of women.

Americans, obviously, cannot eradicate this common denominator of anti-Westernism by renouncing Western civilization. But we can greatly lessen its effectiveness if we rid
ourselves of the prevailing assumption that our way of life,
which is unique even by Western standards, must be regarded
as a norm for all peoples, no matter how much they differ
from us in political, economic, and social development. No
spectacular gestures are required to achieve this purpose. Much
can be done to reassure peoples who are suspicious of the West
by simply avoiding criticism or mockery of customs which
seem strange to us but which, on closer examination, are suited
or at least understandable to other nations. To give only a few
examples which could be endlessly multiplied:

Americans often comment on the uncleanliness of Asians as
compared with the standards of hygiene we have attained with
our running water, bathtubs, soap, toothbrushes, and other
concomitants of what we regard as an advanced civilization.
Yet Asians, by and large, taking their prevailing poverty into
consideration, keep themselves remarkably clean, and regard
our habits of washing as impure. The Hindus, for example,
would not dream of sitting in a bathtub containing water that
has already become dirty. Instead, they pour fresh water over
themselves. They think it unclean to brush their teeth with
toothbrushes, which are used over and over again. Instead,
many brush their teeth with twigs, which can be thrown away
after each usage; and, incidentally, Western dental experts
have come to the conclusion that not only are such twigs better
for the gums and teeth than toothbrushes, but also in some cases
have medicinal qualities.

Or, take the matter of clothes. Americans have thought it
the height of insanity for Arabs living in the hot desert to
wrap themselves up in huge white burnooses. Yet postwar ex-

periments with military equipment under conditions of extreme
heat in the Arizona desert have shown that heavy clothing of
the type worn by the Arabs is actually essential for desert comfort, literally insulating the skin from the broiling tempera-
tures outside and preserving a relatively low body tempera-
ture.

We would win more friends in underdeveloped areas if,
before hastily jumping to conclusions and uttering dogmatic
judgments about other peoples, we would take the time and
use the imagination to understand the circumstances which
may have given rise to the practices that shock or trouble us.
There is no natural law requiring all peoples to look and act
alike. Should such a law ever be invoked, the world would
become a dreary and uninspiring place, shorn of the variations
which we eagerly seek when we embark on journeys to far
lands. Instead of stubbornly demanding conformity to American standards, which in most cases is unattainable because of
lack of money and technical skills, we would find it fruitful
to welcome, show interest in, and encourage the variety of
human experience which contributes to the richness of world
civilization.

Yet while other peoples often criticize us for our alleged
materialism, they at the same time feel admiration, open or
concealed, for the achievements of our economic system. More
and more often, now that the vast disparities between our postwar living standards and those of Western Europe have been
somewhat reduced, we find industrialists and workers of the
Atlantic countries eager to discover the secret of American
productivity. "Britain must not be allowed to become a pic-
turesque Ruritania," says a young Laborite. "We must learn
from you how to modernize our industries so that Britain can
again play a significant role in international economy." "How
do you manage to increase wages and yet sell your goods at
prices the average consumer can buy?" asks the French indus-

trialist. "We must find some way of reducing prices and giving our workers a greater stake in the nation's economy."

But while our friends in Europe, as well as in Asia and Latin America, are eager to learn our methods, they are not always prepared to exchange their more leisurely way of life and their predilection for the hand-wrought products of native craftsmen for the noisy hustle and bustle of American industrial centers and the uniform production of assembly lines. Sooner or later the non-communist nations will have to decide whether they genuinely want greater productivity, even at the sacrifice of some of their cherished traditions — and then make such use of our technological methods as seems best to them; or whether they prefer to continue their present relatively low living standards provided they can enjoy leisure — and then stop envying the United States and criticizing us for our concern with "material" things.

We do not gain much, however, in Asia and the Middle East by comparing our comfortable way of life with that of our leading world competitor, Russia — always in derogatory terms which assume that nothing good can come out of the Soviet system. This approach seldom redounds to our benefit. The peoples of lands which are still less developed than Russia do not find Russian living standards as low as we do. When we tell them that the average annual income in the United States is $1,500 as compared with $300 in Russia, they do not register shock — for they then compare the $300 Russian income with $50 for China, $27 for India, and $30 for Indonesia. They are better aware than we are — and this has been true also of the Soviet leaders since 1917 — of the many practical obstacles which make it difficult, perhaps impossible, for less industrialized nations to match American living standards. For differences in climate, in natural resources, in the health and stamina of peoples, in their level of technical skill, may make the American promise that any nation, if it works hard enough, can become like the United States an unattainable and therefore cruel mirage.

Being aware of these obstacles, the peoples of underdeveloped areas still remain eager to improve their lot. When they hear from us about what the Russians have achieved in a quarter of a century — inadequate as this may seem to us — they find encouragement in the experience of the U.S.S.R. and, far from rejecting it because it is not up to American expectations, they want to study it for the lessons it may hold for them. When we assure these peoples that they have more to learn from us who are technologically in advance of the Russians, they contend that we are so far ahead of them as to discourage imitation. By contrast Russia, which, they agree with us, is still a relatively backward country, has something to teach them because of the very fact that it has but recently emerged from its backwardness, and therefore is closer than we to the conditions and problems they face.

It is essential for us to know what we think of ourselves as well as what other peoples think of us if we are to develop a positive long-term foreign policy. For if our foreign policy is to be based not on wishful thinking but on the realities of world affairs, we shall have to arrive at a more precise understanding of three great issues of our times: (1) the possibility of attaining democracy where it does not exist, and of preserving it where it is already established; (2) the possibility of reconciling our economic concepts and practices with those of other nations; and (3) the possibility of finding a basis for cooperation between the remaining colonial powers and their colonial territories. On each of these issues the United States, a democracy with a powerful modern economy capable of determining the economic destiny of the rest of the world, and with a historic tradition of anti-colonialism, must formulate a coherent program if it is to counter effectively the integrated world program of the U.S.S.R.

4

DEMOCRACY: FOR WHOM
AND HOW MUCH?

At stake in the struggle between democracy and totalitarianism, whatever form it may take, is the possibility of creating in nondemocratic countries conditions favorable to the growth of democratic ideas and institutions. If this possibility exists, and can be effectively used by the Western nations, the next question is whether new democracies can carry out admittedly necessary changes without recourse to the coercive methods of fascist and communist dictatorships.

What can the United States do to promote democracy abroad? Can we expect all nations to achieve democracy in the second half of this century? And what is the content of the democracy we urge other countries to adopt?

All but the most rabid flag-wavers among us would readily admit that American democracy is not free of imperfections, and that a gap, often uncomfortably wide, exists between our professed ideals and our actions. On the whole, however, comparing our way of life with that of other nations, the majority of us feel we have achieved here as satisfactory a relationship between human beings in society as anywhere else in the world at any time in history. This naturally leads us to believe that other peoples would benefit by our example. When they fail to do so, or imitate us only in outward aspects, we are inclined to suspect that they are prevented from espousing democracy by evil-minded leaders hungry for dictatorial power. This is particularly true today when, as a result of our activities all over the globe, our system is directly pitted against the institutions of other peoples, in Germany and Greece, in Korea and Saudi Arabia. If these peoples do not promptly show their admiration for our ideas and practices as compared with their own or, worse, appear to hesitate between our democracy and Russian communism, we tend to regard their doubts and hesitations not as a reflection on their own conditions but on our democratic achievements. This, in turn, challenges us to bolster democratic institutions where they exist, notably through the Marshall Plan in Europe, and to inculcate democracy in formerly anti-democratic societies, as we have tried to do in Germany and Japan since 1945. In our understandable desire to share with other peoples the benefits of democracy as we have developed it here, we sometimes forget that other nations have not had the experience with human freedom which we inherited from the centuries-old struggle of the English people against feudalism and autocracy — a heritage which is shared only by the British dominions, also settled in the first instance by immigrants from England.

Inspired by the example of American history, we expect that every revolution, no matter under what conditions it occurs, will, like our own, usher in without further ado a democracy similar to ours. In this optimistic mood we anticipate a natural and rapid transition from feudalism and autocracy to a Western-type democracy and from a backward agrarian economy to modern industry. Then we are shocked and disappointed to discover that in Russia the autocratic regime of the Czars was followed, with but a brief interval, not by a democratic government but by the dictatorship of the Communists; that in Germany the democratic Weimar Republic turned out to be only a pitiful interlude between Kaiserism and Hitlerism; that the economic modernization of Japan in the latter part of the nineteenth century produced not political democracy but a totalitarian system based on worship of the Emperor as a divinity; that the downfall of Chiang Kai-shek was followed not by the emergence of a liberal regime but by the victory of the Communists; that Marshal Tito's rebellion against Stalin did not overnight transform Yugoslavia into a democratic society; or that the elimination of communism in Spain did not bring the Spanish people the blessings of democratic life and economic prosperity.

The persistent, and understandably appealing, belief that any people can have democracy for the asking, and that if obstacles exist the United States must endeavor to remove them, has caused this country to adopt in world affairs the position of a crusader for democracy. When Woodrow Wilson in 1917 proclaimed the determination of the American people "to make the world safe for democracy," he was voicing a deep-seated national aspiration which continues unabated today. Since 1917, as the tide of totalitarianism has risen all over the globe, some Americans have gone far beyond Woodrow Wilson. They have come to think not only in terms of making the world safe for democracy, but of going into other countries to unseat nondemocratic governments and to create there economic and social conditions that might foster the growth of democratic institutions. Our crusade for democracy has been given seemingly overwhelming justification by the threat first of German nazism and Japanese militarism, then of Russian communism, not only to the democratic way of life but also to the national security of the United States. While it is repugnant to us to think that our propagation of democracy bears the slightest resemblance to the international activities of communism, some of our non-communist critics abroad, while recognizing the vast differences in our methods, have detected similarities in the missionary zeal of the United States and the

U.S.S.R. and in the determination of the two superpowers to win converts to their respective faiths.

In our endeavor to bring about democracy in other countries, what tests can we apply in judging the capacity of peoples living in circumstances far different from ours to copy our institutions? The Western colonial powers had taken the view in the past that the inhabitants of colonies in Asia and Africa were not "ready" for independence and self-government, and would have to be carefully "prepared" to assume democratic responsibilities over a period of time which they were usually reluctant to specify. For this attitude Americans had often criticized the British, French, and other colony-owning nations, taking the view that independence should be granted promptly to all peoples, irrespective of their degree of preparation for self-government. We assumed at that time that any group of human beings, once liberated from colonial rule and given an opportunity to choose freely between the merits of democracy and authoritarianism, would inevitably decide in favor of democracy. Were we right then, or should we revise our concept that Western democracy can be easily adapted to all peoples?

In answering this question, two considerations might be borne in mind. First, our own century has demonstrated that for many individuals freedom seems more of a burden than a privilege. The necessity, intrinsic to the true practice of freedom, of having to make choices between various alternatives, proves onerous to many people who prefer to leave the choice to someone in authority presumed to know what is "best" for the community or the group — *Führer*, or *Duce*, or other leader. In *The Brothers Karamazov*, Dostoevski, writing out of his own experience with conditions under authoritarian Czarism during the nineteenth century but prophetically foreshadowing the totalitarian ideology of the twentieth, paints an unforgettable picture of the process by which some individuals may find satisfaction in surrendering freedom to authority — symbolized by the Grand Inquisitor — and actually feel relief at the thought of no longer having to think and act for themselves. Something of the same feeling must have affected the thousands of Germans who, without at first being subjected to physical danger or even to extensive persuasion, willingly accepted the leadership of Hitler and found satisfaction in being told exactly what to do at home and abroad. In *Darkness at Noon* Arthur Koestler, a former Communist, powerfully describes the shattering struggle of an individual under totalitarian dictatorship to reaffirm his inner freedom. Even in the United States, where we have a deeply rooted tradition of freedom and where the individual is not shy about standing up for his rights and voicing his grievances, the ease with which Senator Joseph McCarthy has influenced public opinion, discouraged criticism of his demagogy, and paralyzed the Department of State, indicates that not all of us in a democratic society have the stamina to challenge encroachments on liberty and to fight for unpopular opinions. Yet without such stamina it is difficult to see how freedom can long flourish in any society. When we are tempted to attribute the rise of nazism in Germany or the survival of communism in Russia to the lack of civic spirit on the part of the Germans or the Russians, we might ask ourselves just how courageous we ourselves are in defending our convictions in a country where opposition does not, as in nazi Germany or communist Russia, involve the danger of imprisonment or death. We must therefore recognize that when we urge peoples who do not have our traditions to assume the obligations of democracy we may be asking them to adopt a course we ourselves, with our uniquely fortunate experience, sometimes find difficult to follow today.

Second, we must remember that until recently the Western nations have tended to apply a double standard in judging democracy. The great English philosopher of liberalism, John

Stuart Mill, in his *Essay on Liberty*, written in the 1860s, advocated complete freedom of "body and mind for the individual, who was to enjoy personal sovereignty, without any restrictions by the state." Mill, however, promptly added that such sovereignty was reserved only for persons of "maturity." In dealing with "barbarians" — a term which for an Englishman of the nineteenth century embraced most of the world outside his island home — it was perfectly proper, according to Mill, to adopt a paternalistic attitude, and to use whatever means seemed best designed to achieve the end of assuring the "barbarians'" well-being as understood, of course, by the advanced civilized nations. This concept, aptly described in relations between the Western powers and their colonial subjects as "the white man's burden," justified dictatorship by the democracies, provided this dictatorship was practiced overseas. Even today the French in Tunisia and Morocco, the Belgians in the Belgian Congo, justify continued tutelage of colonial peoples on the ground that they are not prepared for self-government — even though self-government has been granted under United Nations sponsorship to Libya, whose peoples are less advanced than the Tunisians.

The tendency of many Westerners to believe that the peoples of backward areas under their rule can quite properly be treated in a nondemocratic way, purportedly for their own good, makes it more difficult for us to denounce the Russians for dealing in nondemocratic ways with their peoples, some of whom by our own standards are still relatively backward. There is no question that the Russians, while constantly criticizing the "oppression" of the colonial powers, treat not only their own "colonials" in Central Asia but all the population of the U.S.S.R. in a ruthless manner. But it does not help the cause of democracy, when pointing out the evil-doings of the Russians, to claim that the Western nations have never tolerated cruelty and oppression in their colonies. On this score the testimony of some of the colonial peoples would not always harmonize with that of the colonial administrators when the record of the past two centuries is reviewed. Colonial nationalists, moreover, contend that if there is to be dictatorship, then native dictators, no matter how cruel and oppressive, are easier to bear and more likely to be overthrown than Western rulers backed by modern weapons which in the past were not available to the colonial population.

We must also bear in mind that the United States has proved far less intolerant of non-nazi and non-communist dictatorships, no matter how much their restrictions on freedom resemble those of the Nazis or the Communists, than of nazism and communism. It is not uncommon to hear well-intentioned and fair-minded Americans say on a visit to Argentina or Spain, the Dominican Republic or Thailand: "Well, after all, these people have had no experience with freedom, and they really need a dictator."

When this seeming discrimination between dictatorships is pointed out, the immediate answer is that there is a vast difference between Russia and the Dominican Republic, or China and Thailand — as indeed there is. Russia and China constitute a threat to the security of the United States, while the Dominican Republic and Thailand cannot, under any imaginable circumstances, prove a danger to this country. This argument carries weight in terms of world politics. But it tends to weaken our crusade for democracy by revealing that the United States has no objection to dictatorships so long as they do not affect our own interests, and may not be as eager to press for reforms in Spain and the Dominican Republic, in Thailand and Argentina, as it is in Russia and China, Poland and Bulgaria. Our double standard on the issue of democracy may seem to be justified at the present time by the exigencies of the cold war. But it may not prove altogether convincing to countries whom we are urging to adopt democracy. It is well to recall the confusion created in the 1930s when Britain and France, while clinging to their colonial possessions, berated Italy for attempting to carve out a colony for itself in Ethiopia — an attitude that Baron Aloisi, Italy's representative to the League of Nations, then described as the application of "two weights and two measures."

When we prescribe democracy for other nations, we do so not merely because we prefer democracy to totalitarianism, but because we sincerely believe that only democracies can effect necessary changes by peaceful means and thereby avoid the danger of revolutions which might serve the purposes of Russia and communism. No responsible person who has ever had firsthand experience with revolution would want to wish such experience for friendly nations. Yet in many of the countries we are now proud to count among our friends, the democratic conditions we admire and support were brought about in the first instance by resort to force — the revolt of Oliver Cromwell in England in the seventeenth century, the French Revolution of 1789, the uprisings of Garibaldi and Mazzini in Italy in the 1860s. The fact that these revolutionary changes now occupy honored niches in history and that the governments they brought to power have, through long acceptance, become respectable does not alter their original character. Nor is it irrelevant to recall that the French Revolution, in its time, provoked in the United States and Britain something of the same revulsion which is now felt in the West about the revolutions of Russia and China.

But looking solely at our own segment of history in this century, we cannot fail to notice that in many nations attempts of more or less democratic governments to make changes by peaceful means have so far produced not the reforms we ourselves believe are essential for their future well-being — such as land reform in Italy, Iran, or Egypt — but slowdowns or stalemates whose continuation may merely intensify the eventual explosion of public resentment. It was to break such a stale-mate that Kemal Atatürk established an authoritarian govern-ment in Turkey, which twenty years later evolved into a limited form of democracy, and Gen. Mohammed Naguib, brushing aside ineffectual and clashing political parties, set up a military dictatorship in Egypt, determined to carry out land reform and other economic and social measures.

Gradualism is both desirable and commendable. But it seems to be effective only in societies where the political leaders have achieved sufficient maturity to realize the need for reconciling conflicting interests and have developed a sufficient degree of disinterestedness to carry through changes beneficial to the community as a whole, even though they disturb vested inter-ests. If this is true, then we can hardly expect to see even the rudiments of democratic institutions in countries where po-litical education has just begun and where national leaders, irrespective of party, still think primarily in terms of the inter-ests of family, clan, or sect, not of the community, as is still true today in the Middle East, Asia, and Latin America.

In such countries, which have not yet come under com-munist rule but cannot by any stretch of the imagination be described as democratic according to our standards, the intro-duction of literacy, the education of citizens in the first princi-ples of democratic procedure, and any improvement that can be made in economic and social well-being, may eventually help to clear the ground for the growth of democratic institu-tions. Such reforms, however, may be more effectively carried out by intelligent authoritarian regimes like that of Kemal Atatürk in Turkey or of General Naguib in Egypt than by feudal oligarchs masquerading as democrats in order to gain American financial aid. Literacy, education, and material im-provements, however, cannot be achieved overnight. Nor do they necessarily guarantee democracy, as we saw when the Germans — literate, educated, and enjoying a standard of living higher than that of most Europeans — turned with little resistance to a ruthless form of totalitarianism. Democracy is a delicate plant. It requires the proper climate and nurture if it is not to wither in the heat of life-and-death controversies. Little is gained if politically underdeveloped countries, at our behest, hastily throw up the façade of democracy, such as elections and parliamentary assemblies, but fail to underpin it with the practices of genuine democratic life. Façade democracy can be found in many countries under one-party non-communist dictatorships. Take, for example, the 1951 presidential election in Portugal from which all candidates except the one favored by the government were eliminated; or Argentina, where Perón "sacrificed" himself by running once more for the presidency in 1951, after having suppressed all opportunity for genuine political opposition. But while we regard elections in the "people's democracies" of Russia, Eastern Europe, or China a mockery of democracy, we seem less troubled by the mere outward obeisance of non-communist dictatorships to the rituals associated with democratic institutions.

More important than the trappings of democracy is the sense of responsibility of political leaders in a given country. If we feel that the exigencies of the cold war justify American military and financial aid to dictatorships, whether anti-Communist like that of General Franco or Communist like that of Marshal Tito, then we can no longer apply the litmus test of whether or not all our new friends are dedicated to democracy. The most we can ask, after assuring ourselves that they will in good faith stay on our side and not go over to Russia should the cold war become hot, is whether their leaders really intend to improve the lot of the people, by whatever means they choose, or plan to make use of our aid merely to maintain themselves in power. This is a legitimate question for us to ask, not from the point of view of our ideals — for presently we have decided to bend our ideals here and there in order to obtain strategic advantages — but from the point of view of our own future security. For if the political leaders with whom we deal should prove adamant in resisting all changes in their own countries and utilize the prestige of our support as well as the strength of the armaments we furnish them to suppress all political opposition, then any revolution that may subsequently occur will be directed at least as much against the United States as against the native dictator we have enlisted on our side. Looking at the situation strictly in terms of security, and leaving faith in democracy aside, such an eventuality might well jeopardize our expectations of building a stable and internally healthy coalition against Russia and communism.

Some Americans, realizing this danger, contend that when existing governments in countries the United States wants as allies are unwilling or incapable of carrying out reforms we deem to be necessary, we should undertake to carry out such reforms either by exerting pressure on the political leaders or even by direct action of our own. Direct political intervention, however, is fraught with danger. First, it contradicts our claim that we deal with other nations in a democratic manner, as contrasted with Nazi conquests or the coercive methods of the U.S.S.R., which does not hesitate to discard governments that do not comply with its bidding, replacing them with authorities of its own choice.

But second, and over the long run more disturbing, the reforms we undertake ourselves may kill off the political initiative which, presumably, we should try to foster in countries unfamiliar with democratic practices. This paternalistic way of doing things would merely confirm nondemocratic peoples in the belief that all acts of benevolence fall like manna from heaven, with no need for exertion on their part — irrespective, to take the case of Japan, of whether the source of reform be a divine Emperor or the United States occupation authorities.

Gen. Douglas MacArthur introduced some excellent changes in Japan, notably land reform, extension of trade-union rights, and new opportunities for women in political life. Some of these reforms had long been advocated by the Japanese Socialists but, because they eventually came through American fiat rather than through a struggle among the Japanese political parties, the Socialists had neither the opportunity to test their strength in a genuine political contest nor the benefit of being credited with the improvements they had previously urged.

Reform by foreign intervention may well be the shortest road to democratization, but it is the least reliable. For reforms identified with foreign rule — especially if it is foreign military occupation — will be viewed with suspicion even by its beneficiaries, and deeply resented by its opponents, who will seize the first opportunity to junk them in an emotional appeal to anti-foreign sentiment. Such reforms will have no roots in the country's political life. And the foreigner who by-passes native political forces with the commendable aim of speeding the growth of democracy, will discover that instead he has emasculated the country's budding democratic aspirations.

Thus in its efforts to make the world over in its own democratic image, the United States seems confronted with the dilemma of "damned if you do and damned if you don't." Yet it is no longer possible for us to wash our hands altogether both of democracies and of dictatorships, and some decision or other will be incumbent upon us unless we want to surrender the political battlefield to Russia by default.

Since the United States, in Yugoslavia and Spain, not to speak of other nations, has decided to subordinate its insistence on democracy to political and military requirements, we can no longer demand that these countries comply with democratic standards as a condition of receiving our aid. The best thing for us to do now is to recognize frankly that many peoples, for a variety of reasons, are not yet prepared for democratic institutions, and to stop proclaiming the unadulterated "democratic" character of the coalition we are building. We may also find it advisable to be a little less rigid in passing judgment on the exact percentage of democratic content in the institutions of countries which are still struggling to stay neutral, such as India and Indonesia, and even of our actual or potential enemies.

Since the concept of democracy makes it impossible for us to depose existing governments by force or conspiracy, the most effective thing we can do to promote democratic institutions is to practice democracy at home as effectively as we can.

The challenge of nazism, fascism, and communism has had the beneficial effect of forcing us to reexamine our own political system to make sure that we try to mend all the chinks in our armor which might conceivably inspire hostile propaganda. Until we had been thus challenged, we were inclined to view crime, political corruption, juvenile delinquency, and other recognized weaknesses of our society, as well as demagogy about foreign policy, as unpleasant but inevitable evils of democracy — part of the price we had to pay for the advantages of individual freedom. But now that our society is daily on display, subject to the scrutiny not only of our admiring eyes but also of the critical, or even hostile, gaze of other nations, we have suddenly realized the urgent need for a house cleaning. The impact of the Kefauver committee investigations, which did not reveal much we had not known before but succeeded, because of the new medium of television, in dramatizing the network of crime in the midst of which we have been living with a remarkable degree of complacency, was greatly enhanced by our realization that, tolerant as we might be about its revelations, our friends and enemies abroad would not be inclined to take so lenient a view.

As Adlai Stevenson well said in Richmond, Virginia, on

September 21, 1952, this does not mean that we should improve our democracy "just because if we do not we shall give Soviet Russia a propaganda weapon. . . . We must do right for right's sake alone." But our increasing awareness of the inextricable connection between what we do at home and what we do abroad has spurred us into strengthening those features of our democracy which had begun to sag or had never developed up to the level of our proclaimed ideals. There is little doubt, for example, that our practice of civil liberties, notably with respect to our Negro fellow citizens, has been greatly accelerated and broadened in an effort to establish here standards of interracial and intergroup conduct which would make it possible for us to champion democracy in other areas of the world without mental reservations.

America can also make it clear to countries receiving our aid that, while we have no desire of becoming king-and-cabinet makers, we definitely prefer democracy to dictatorships (even those dictatorships which invoke the name of God for their justification); freedom to suppression; constant efforts to bring about equality of economic and social conditions to the maintenance of blatant inequality; attempts, no matter how modest, to improve living standards to the persistence of economic stagnation. Nonintervention does not mean indifference. Respect for the rights of other peoples to choose and overthrow their governments does not mean political agnosticism on our part. If we have political convictions, let us make them manifest. We must not mock or criticize the institutions of other countries until we have at least made an effort to understand how they came about, and try to discover whether they could be altered by peaceful means. But we need not leave any nation in a state of uncertainty about our preference, even if the times and the circumstances do not permit immediate compliance with these preferences. We can thus preserve our political integrity without trespassing on that of others.

Similarly, in the economic sphere, America can indicate that its main preoccupation, inspired by a long tradition of concern for the underprivileged, is to foster the alleviation, even if only gradual, of the poverty, hunger, illiteracy, ill-health, and racial discrimination which today, in a period of vast scientific achievement that makes change appear not only possible but essential, remain the lot of two-thirds of mankind and continue to feed the fires of communism. It is significant that communism has proved most ineffective in countries like Britain, the Dominions, and the Scandinavian nations which had taken steps to broaden the economic and social base of political democracy. But we must realize that merely "wishing does not make it so." America can, and must, give aid to other nations which are seeking, often at our urging, to emerge from their state of backwardness. We can give them the "know-how"; but they alone can decide on the "know-why" of their search for improvement. They may be eager to adopt, or adapt, our techniques, but we must not interfere with the ultimate purposes to which these techniques will be applied. While it would please and reassure many of us to see the nations we aid introduce free-enterprise methods, our own traditional willingness to experiment should help us to understand their desire to follow the course they consider best, and make it possible for us to accept the prospect that other peoples may find salvation in ways different from our own.

If we who so fervently believe in freedom can accept the idea of free choice for other peoples, then we can do a great deal by offering to share our scientific knowledge, technical skills, managerial capacity, and other gifts in which we excel and which are still rare in many lands. To do an effective job we must keep ideology in the background as much as possible, avoid missionary zeal, and again, as in the political sphere, let our deeds speak louder than our words. Above all, we must become accustomed to the idea that other peoples may choose ways of life different from our own without thereby indicating hostility toward the United States. Today we tend to view other nations' experiments with alarm and suspicion, just as America was once viewed with alarm and suspicion by the older, more rigid nations of Europe. Perhaps the greatest contribution we could make to the expansion of democracy would be simply to live up to our often proclaimed determination that every people has a right to develop according to its own aspirations, provided it does not encroach on the rights of its neighbors to do likewise.

Any form of self-government, no matter how rudimentary, presupposes national independence. Yet just as the individual can no longer be sovereign in the sense in which Mill wrote about liberty a hundred years ago, so the nation can no longer be sovereign within the community of nations. The United States, by its own actions, notably by our participation in the United Nations and other international agencies and most dramatically by our 1950 decision to place American armed forces under the sponsorship of the UN in Korea, recognizes that the day of unrestricted national sovereignty has passed. This country, which only a quarter of a century ago still asserted its sovereign right to remain isolated, has now swung to the other extreme, of insisting that other nations accept, in the UN, our concept of what is good for the world community.

Our intentions are excellent. We want to make sure that the UN will resist aggression wherever it may occur, and that the machinery of collective security can be put into action without delay. But because of our prevailing desire to find quick remedies for troublesome situations, we are apt to become impatient, to rush things, to address nations which in World War II struggled bitterly to retain independence, like France and Norway, or have only recently achieved it, like India, in peremptory tones; and to insist that, without further ado, they "integrate or die," or decide whether they are "with us or against us." By a curious paradox, the United States, which before 1945 seemed to epitomize national resistance to international cooperation, now seems ready to curtail the sovereignty of fellow members of the UN to achieve collective security.

Our own very recent reluctance to accept international commitments and our current insistence that we are free to act as a sovereign state on such matters as tariffs and immigration should make us a little less impatient with those of our present or potential friends who do not unquestioningly accept our every suggestion. Being new to world politics, we are not always aware that our paramount economic strength puts us in a position where a single decision on our part can spell ruin for other nations — for example, our decision to reduce the world price of tin in 1951 threw the economy of Malaya into confusion. The United States can make a distinct contribution to world stability by realizing the impact of its own power, and by acting like an intelligent, not a heedless, giant, careful not to throw his weight around in a reckless way. In a world riven by the struggle between the two superpowers, no nation, even if it was but recently great and influential like Britain, and least of all if it is small and relatively weak, like Iran or Poland, can hope to maintain its freedom of decision, its territorial integrity, and other prerequisites of traditional national independence, which in turn assure the survival of self-government, unless it can reliably depend on the protection of a strong international organization where no great power — not even a benevolent United States — seeks to play a domineering role. Democracy begins at home. But it must also be practiced in the United Nations' forum.

The United Nations must not be viewed as an agency for the advancement only of our political and economic concepts. Nor should it be used solely, or even primarily, as an instrument of collective security against military aggression. It must, above all, be a protective association against undue demands by all great powers on small nations, whether these demands, which we ourselves once labeled "imperialistic," concern strategic raw materials, bases, compliance with given ideologies, or any kind of intervention in internal affairs.

If we want to see democracy achieved throughout the world, yet recognize that this country cannot enforce democracy on other peoples without jeopardizing its own democratic character, we could urge the establishment of minimum international standards of internal political conduct which would then be invoked not by the United States but by the United Nations. In endeavoring to set such standards, we would soon discover, as we did in the United Nations Commission on Human Rights, the great divergence that exists between the various UN members with respect to political, economic, and social development. We would also discover the need to make allowances for such divergence, just as we make allowances for various age levels in our schools, instead of expecting that all nations must be fitted, without qualifications and without delay, into the Procrustean bed of our unique political experience.

It would become clear to us, too, that democratic institutions and procedures can be a hollow sham unless they are firmly based on economic and social conditions adapted to the needs of modern industrial society which has now become the goal of all nations. As Sydney Bailey, secretary of the Hansard Society in London, has well said: "The parliamentary system, by itself, cannot guarantee a higher standard of living. Parliaments do not grow rice, nor cabinets construct irrigation works. Yet if these things are not done, the people may lose patience with parliamentary institutions and demand some alternative methods of government."

One of our greatest assets in promoting democracy abroad —

an asset of which we have hitherto made inadequate use — is that the United States, in the past quarter of a century, has itself undergone vast economic and social changes tantamount to a revolution. Instead of hiding our light under a bushel, we should openly proclaim the scope and significance of this revolution, and apply its lessons in our foreign policy.

5

OUR UNADMITTED REVOLUTION

H ESITANCY about carrying over into world affairs the economic and social changes that have taken place here
during the past quarter of a century often distorts and frus-
trates our foreign policy. Spokesmen of both our political
parties deplore the rule of small feudal-minded cliques in non-
communist countries of the Middle East, or Asia, or Latin
America, and proclaim the blessings of democracy. Yet often
these same spokesmen give the impression that any attempt, no
matter how modest or how urgently needed, to alter the existing situation in Italy or Iran, in Indo-China or Guatemala, may
generate a ferment favorable to communist designs and must
therefore be deplored. In Latin America the desire to preserve
"order" and check communism has led us to put armaments in
the hands of dictators who use these armaments to suppress all
groups which advocate change.

The paradoxical result is that the United States, while leading
a crusade for democracy against dictatorship, has come to the
conclusion that the maintenance in power of General Franco
in Spain or Chiang Kai-shek on Formosa, of Emperor Bao Dai
in Indo-China or Dr. Syngman Rhee in South Korea, is essential
to the security of the United States. Then, before we know it,
the impression gains ground that, since Russia and communism

are inimical to the American way of life, support of Franco, Chiang, and others is synonymous with the survival of our own institutions and ideals. The next step in this chain of reasoning is the assumption that any American, let alone any foreigner, who questions such a course is disloyal — disloyal not to Franco or Chiang but to the American government, and acts suspiciously like a subversive.

This line of thought has made it increasingly difficult since 1945 for American officials charged with the making of foreign policy to arrive at reasoned judgments about world affairs for fear of attacks on their loyalty. It has also bewildered our actual or potential friends in other countries. They are at a loss to understand why the United States persists in defending institutions and practices it would not tolerate at home and appears to oppose economic and social changes which have long been a commonplace here, while at the same time constantly demanding that other nations "modernize" themselves and benefit by the lessons of American technological experience. Can feudal landowners, our friends ask, be expected to introduce land reforms? Can industrialists who in the past have shown no sense of social responsibility and have fought trade unions be expected to favor fair-minded social legislation and treat labor in a twentieth-century spirit? Is it wise, they say, for the United States to urge "free enterprise" on Western European nations where capitalism has long been shackled by various restrictions or on underdeveloped lands where capitalism has hitherto appeared either in the guise of foreign exploitation of raw materials or native profiteering — particularly since the United States itself, in recent decades, has profoundly modified the system of untrammeled "free enterprise" which it is offering other nations as a model for imitation? Do Americans, our friends want to know, expect non-communist nations to copy its present economic and social institutions, or those it had in the nineteenth century?

The basic problem in our discussions of economic and social changes abroad is that, long after we have absorbed into our society alterations of the American system which could be described as "revolutionary," we continue to talk as if our institutions had remained unaltered since the early days of capitalist development. Our friends know, from firsthand experience here, that in the past quarter of a century the United States has introduced many fundamental changes: from recognition of the role of labor unions in an industrial society to social security, from increased Federal aid for education to an elaborate program of farm support. Yet instead of taking credit for these changes, initiated by New Deal and Fair Deal Democratic administrations but carried out with the approval and active support of independents and many Republicans, we seem to feel uneasy about them, and some of us still decry them as "creeping socialism." It is as if we had produced a new system within the chrysalis of the old, but felt restrained by some unavowed fear from shedding the chrysalis and emerging openly in our new guise, proud, not ashamed, of our capacity for self-renewal. Our seeming preference to be judged in other lands by what we once were rather than by what we are today seems inspired by a nostalgic hope on the part of some Americans that, if only political power would change hands, "the good old days" would return and the changes carried out since the 1930s would be erased.

Yet it is these changes which, in the opinion of our friends abroad, made it possible for the United States to effect an orderly, peaceful transformation from the anarchy of laissez-faire society, with everyone for himself and the devil take the hindmost, into a modern industrial nation where all citizens feel concern for the well-being of the community as a whole. These changes, if vigorously publicized outside our borders, would most eloquently convince other nations that the United States, to quote John Strachey, former Secretary of War in

Britain's Labor government who once admired communism and vigorously criticized this country, is now not only the greatest capitalist power of the world but that its capitalism is "in rapid and progressive development."

Obviously, there is always room for improvement in every society, including our own. But Americans have every reason to feel pride, not defeatism, about what has been accomplished in this country to improve living standards, conditions of work, opportunities for health and education, housing, and possibilities for creative leisure, and to give the masses of our population a greater sense of security about continuity of employment and subsistence in case of unemployment, accident, or ill-health. Instead of fretting about the "socialist" implications of these accomplishments, we should admit that the United States, at mid-twentieth century, has carried out a bloodless economic and social revolution, and is qualified to act as the world's standard-bearer of economic and social democracy. It is nothing short of fantastic that this country, which has rapidly and imaginatively adapted its economy not only to technological changes but also to changes in human relationships, should permit itself to be regarded abroad as a bulwark of unreformed capitalism, and thus fail to wrest the banner of revolution from the hands of Russia which, whatever its internal achievements, still has a backward economy compared to ours both in technical and human terms.

The chief obstacles to utilizing the economic and social changes we have wrought here as an asset in our foreign policy is the apparent ambivalence between the urge for progressivism felt by large sectors of our population and reflected in programs launched by the Executive, on the one hand, and the persistent conservatism of the majority in Congress on the other. As Roscoe Drummond, chief of the Washington News Bureau of *The Christian Science Monitor,* wrote in late 1951, "While the country has been consistently electing New Deal Presidents, it has, for the past 12 years, been consistently electing anti-New Deal Congresses." If this Congressional trend toward conservatism should now be matched by conservatism in the Executive, American foreign-policy makers will be confronted with the perplexing question of how a predominantly conservative-minded people — if such we are — can effectively assume leadership in a world where revolutionary ferment is at work, and guide other nations intelligently toward peaceful change. This question seems all the more perplexing because American businessmen, for the most part, continue to demonstrate great inventiveness and adaptability and welcome, indeed encourage, changes in methods or production and distribution which mark the United States as the opposite of "conservative." Somehow or other, we must infuse the forward-looking spirit of our business and industrial leaders into the economic and social thinking of Congress, and reconcile our willingness to accept technological change with our seeming reluctance to welcome social change. Then we shall be able to present abroad a more coherent picture of what we regard as our most promising domestic achievements and offer these achievements more convincingly as a model for other nations to follow.

Our so-far-unadmitted revolution has many facets. Perhaps the most striking of all, as our friends are prompt to note, is the remarkable transformation that has occurred between 1929 and 1951 in the distribution of our national income — a transformation which we, the world's greatest addicts of the art of advertising, have done little to advertise abroad. In the thirty-first annual report of the National Bureau of Economic Research, *Looking Forward,** Professor Arthur F. Burns of Columbia University gave figures which, if broadcast throughout the world, would promptly alter the prevailing concept of

* Arthur F. Burns, *Looking Forward*, 31st Annual Report, National Bureau of Economic Research, May 1951.

the United States as a land of arrested economic development, the leader of conservative opposition to revolution, and restore it to the role for which it has been historically cast — the role of leadership in economic change by peaceful democratic methods.

In 1929, Professor Burns points out, "the highest 5 per cent of the income recipients obtained 34 per cent of the total disposable income of individuals — that is, the total of personal income, inclusive of any capital gains but after deducting federal income tax payments. By 1939 their share had dropped to 27 per cent of total income, and by 1946 to 15 per cent. Since 1946 the wide structure of the income distribution does not seem to have changed materially, so that we may regard the distribution in that year as roughly representative of current conditions. If we now compare 1949 and 1946, we find that the share going to the top 5 per cent group declined 16 points. Had perfect equality of income been attained in 1946 the share would have dropped from 34 to 5 per cent, that is, by 29 points. In other words, the income share of the top 5 per cent stratum dropped 16 points out of a maximum possible drop of 29 points; so that, on the basis of this yardstick, we may be said to have traveled in a bare two decades over half the distance separating the 1929 distribution from a perfectly egalitarian distribution. If we turn to the top 1 instead of the two top 5 per cent, the results are still more striking. The share of the top 1 per cent group in total income was 19.1 per cent in 1929 and 7.7 per cent in 1946. Since the share of this group dropped 11.4 points out of a total drop of 18.1 points, we have traveled since 1929 on the basis of this yardstick almost two-thirds of the distance towards absolute income equality."

These conclusions, Professor Burns contends, indicate that "if we are to look forward constructively to a material reduction of income inequalities in the future, we must seek to attain it principally by raising the productivity of those at the bottom of the income scale rather than by transferring income from the high to the poor. . . . The paramount source of the rising living standards of our workers and farmers has always been an increasing volume of production, and in the years ahead it bids fair to become the only source." And he reemphasizes this point by stating, when he discusses the problems that may arise in an economy geared for long-term defense: "If the rightful aspirations of workers and farmers for better living standards are to be realized with a minimum of social unrest, it will become necessary to strive for even greater increases in productivity than have ruled in the past."

Professor Burns, moreover, does not shy away from the fact that altered economic and social conditions necessitate greater participation by government than has existed in the past, or assume that any rigid formula defining the respective roles of government and private enterprise can be evolved in a period of rapid internal and external changes. "The broad trend of development in a progressive economy," he says, "is towards sharply increasing emphasis on the service industries, and the government is merely one of the major channels through which the public's demand for service is satisfied. An economy undergoing rapid industrialization and urbanization increases the interdependence of men — their exposure to the wisdom and enterprise, also the folly and indolence, of their neighbors. Social and economic problems arise that cannot be handled adequately by private enterprise. With the spread of political democracy the demand increases for collective action to broaden educational opportunity, to improve sanitation and health, reduce slums, conserve natural resources, eliminate or regulate private monopoly, supervise banks and insurance companies, protect workers against the hazards of unemployment, and so on. Thus the line separating private enterprise and governmental responsibility is constantly re-drawn, the range of governmental activities broadens, and a 'mixed economy' comes into being."

The key phrases in Professor Burns's analysis — "the rightful aspirations of workers and farmers for better living standards," "a progressive economy," "the spread of political democracy," "mixed economy" and "collective action" to broaden opportunities and improve social conditions for all — are in harmony with the concepts of mid-twentieth-century society held by the non-communist parties of Western Europe such as the Labor parties of Britain and Norway, the Socialists or Social Democrats of Sweden and Denmark, of France and West Germany, and the social-minded Catholic groups from the Mouvement Républicain Populaire in France to the left wing of Premier de Gasperi's Christian Democrats and even the more outspoken elements of the clergy in Spain who are urging improvements in the living standards of the workers. Meanwhile, the Labor and Socialist parties of Europe have moved closer to middle-of-the-road thinking in the United States as they have assumed responsibility for government, in Britain and Norway, or have come to play an increasingly important part in political life, as in France and West Germany.

At their eighth international conference in Frankfort, in June 1951, the Socialists of twenty-two countries established a new Socialist International whose program is not very far apart from the analysis of economic conditions and prospects in the United States as outlined by Professor Burns. The Socialist program is still critical of capitalism — but it is important to bear in mind that the capitalism it criticizes is the old-fashioned capitalism of Western Europe, frozen in the obsolete molds of the nineteenth century, "feudalism rather than capitalism," to quote an American ECA official — not the reformed and reinvigorated capitalism of the United States. The Socialists, moreover, recognize that the "class struggle," originally waged under the banner of Karl Marx almost entirely on behalf of factory workers, has lost its strictly "class" character now that the demand for improvements in economic and social conditions is supported by constantly broadening groups of the population. Having had an opportunity to put their ideas about nationalization to the test, the Socialists, some of whom have been disillusioned about the effectiveness of this method in increasing productivity, reducing costs of production and thereby raising living standards, now declare that nationalization is not a prerequisite of socialism, and that there is room for peaceful cooperation between public undertakings and private enterprise.

The Socialists proclaim their ineradicable opposition to communism, and assert that individual freedom and human liberties are their paramount objectives. They contend, however, that the most powerful safeguard against communism is not military preparedness but unremitting effort to improve the economic and social bases of society. On this issue there would seem to be no conflict between the European Labor and Socialist parties, on the one hand, and those Americans who, by supporting the Marshall Plan for Europe and the Point Four program of technical assistance for underdeveloped countries, have demonstrated their belief that if communism is to be defeated without the destruction of war it will be necessary to improve and keep on improving the lot of human beings now living under substandard conditions and therefore vulnerable to Communist promises and pressures.

Thus, looking at the United States in its real lineaments, not the lineaments of the reactionary monster painted by communist propaganda, our friends abroad see it as the most advanced, socially progressive country in the world — all the more advanced because Americans command the technological skills to translate what to Socialists elsewhere are still glorious dreams into concrete achievements. What surprises them is that the United States seems slow to recognize this image of itself as it appears to others and, instead, seems to take inexplicable satisfaction in conveying to the world an image reminiscent of the incongruous reflections given back by those distorting mirrors which delight crowds at beach resorts. If we sometimes wonder why other peoples do not see us as we think we really are, we might ask whether we ourselves are not the creators, consciously or unconsciously, of the distortions to which we vehemently object.

Today, when some of our top business leaders represented in the National Association of Manufacturers urge Western European capitalists to speed up the fight against communism by modifying Old World capitalism and adopting the essentials of the American brand of free enterprise, they stress greater competition, higher productivity, broader "consumptivity," rising living standards, and growing economic strength, as contrasted with the cartels, monopolies, and other restrictions on production and consumption which, they have somewhat belatedly acknowledged, characterize the European type of capitalism. But they still say little or nothing of the far-reaching economic and social changes of the past quarter of a century that in the United States facilitated the peaceful transition from old-fashioned capitalism to the new productivity and "consumptivity" of the mid-twentieth century.

Yet one of the facets of our unadmitted revolution which most strikes foreign visitors, even those who are deeply conservative, is the extent to which participation by the government in the development and conservation of the nation's natural resources has come to be accepted by this country's free-enterprise supporters among businessmen, as well as by other groups of the population, notably in the states of our West. Great public undertakings for the benefit of the community such as the Tennessee Valley Authority, the Grand Coulee, the Hoover Dam, the Colorado–Big Thompson development are now taken for granted by Americans who in the twentieth century have gradually come to identify social responsibility and economic opportunity with political democ-

racy. The most rugged individualists among us see nothing
revolutionary in projects of irrigation, hydroelectric power
generation, and forest conservation in which the Federal government plays a more or less important part. And for people
abroad, in Asia and the Middle East and Africa, as well as in
Europe, TVA has become the most significant symbol of what
is best in modern America. It therefore comes as a surprise to
our friends in Western Europe when we who have accepted
the practice of government participation in so many sectors
of our economic life, criticize the governments of Britain,
France, West Germany, or the Scandinavian countries for taking a hand in the development of their far more limited natural
resources which must be more carefully husbanded than ours
for the satisfaction of their peoples' needs.

Nor do the majority of Americans see anything revolutionary today, whatever they may have felt in the 1930s, in the
increasing participation of labor unions in national affairs;
in such measures as social security and old-age pensions; or in
various proposals, some of them supported by members of the
medical profession, for insurance arrangements that would provide aid to families of modest means in case of prolonged or
chronic illness. These developments, while still sometimes de-
rided as unhealthy manifestations of the "welfare state," are
recognized by thoughtful citizens, whether Republicans or
Democrats, as consistent with the growth of social responsibility in a democratic industrial society. Our friends in Western
Europe are therefore all the more surprised to find that even
some progressive-minded Americans look askance at the programs and activities of Labor and Socialist parties, especially
when these parties, notably the British Laborites, succeed in
coming to power. During the postwar years, when American
officials on the European continent were asked why the United
States appeared to shun Socialists and displayed a marked preference for conservative and sometimes outright reactionary

parties, the almost invariable answer was: "Well, how can we support socialism (in West Germany, France, Italy, Japan, or anywhere else) when we oppose it at home?"

Few Americans advocate out-and-out socialism for the United States, and the Socialist party here, long headed by the eloquent Norman Thomas, has in recent years lost the small ground it had once won — although it has consoled itself with the thought that many of its ideas have gradually permeated the thinking of non-Socialists. It is important, however, that we should understand the reasons why socialism has won support in Europe, and not keep on confusing the Socialists, who are determined foes of communism and oppose violence and dictatorship, with the Communists. For if we are to help Europe modernize its economy and achieve higher levels of productivity and social well-being, we shall have to work, as American labor leaders have long recognized, not only with industrialists, but also with the trade unions and with the Socialist, Labor, and progressive Catholic parties.

This will prove even more important in our efforts to achieve cooperation with the nations of Asia, the Middle East, and Latin America, which are still in the early stages of industrialization, and where the development programs we ourselves advocate, because of lack of responsible local capitalists, will have to be initiated by governments if the economic and social interests of the population are to be safeguarded from profiteering and exploitation. In the underdeveloped areas we not only have to ask ourselves whether the economic and social changes which seem necessary to combat communism can be carried out by peaceful democratic means, but also whether we should help to perpetuate the remnants of colonial rule or throw our support to the side of nationalist movements which demand both political independence and economic reforms.

6

ARRESTED
ANTI-COLONIALISM

THE problems we face in winning friends among the Asian peoples are profoundly different in scope and character from those we face in our relations with Western Europe. Difficult as it may often be for us to understand the British and Germans, the French and Italians, we at least have in common with them the traditions and beliefs that constitute Western civilization. Like the nations of Western Europe, we have experienced the Industrial Revolution which we have carried, in this century, far beyond the point it had reached in the Old World. We differ, and shall continue to differ, with West Europeans on many controversial issues. But we share in their heritage of the past, and they, in turn, share in our current development.

Asia, by contrast, is for most of us an alien world in which we have had little or no direct part. We regard it with that mixture of curiosity and suspicion that unknown things usually arouse in human beings. In communicating with Asia we must start practically from scratch. This is particularly true of Southeast Asia and of the Moslem countries with which we have had very limited contacts as compared with China and Japan. Our highly industrialized society, driven by faith in the efficacy of political democracy and in the effectiveness of material action, must find ways of making itself understood and appreciated by societies which are still at the stage of backward agrarianism; whose people have until recently been governed either by Western colonial administrators or by native feudal rulers; where electricity, public-health measures, adequate nutrition, primitive sanitation, and the simplest kinds of mechanical tools are for the most part unfamiliar and unavailable.

In the countries of Asia — and this is true also of the Middle East and even more of certain areas of Africa — headlong attempts to introduce Western-type democracy may produce chaos. Well-intentioned efforts to install machine civilization may wreck the existing economy and create dangerous social maladjustments that would foster the activities either of groups of the extreme Right, often fanatically religious, or of the extreme Left, usually fanatically Communist. If Americans are well advised to think twice before they tell Europe what to do, even greater circumspection is prescribed for the propaganda activities of the United States in Asia.

Our task in Asia is further complicated by the role the United States is believed to have hitherto played with respect to colonialism and the change in emphasis it is thought to have made since 1945. If there is one single thing for which this country has been known and admired in Asia it is for the revolt of the young American republic against British colonial rule in 1776. It would be unrealistic to compare the American revolution, carried out by a literate, politically experienced, and economically prosperous population, with the nationalist movements in Indonesia or Iran. But this act of liberation almost two hundred years ago has reverberated throughout the areas which in our times have been held as colonies by the great powers of Western Europe. Its impact was reinforced by the emancipation of the Negro slaves in 1861, with the result that the names of Washington and Lincoln have become indelibly imprinted on the minds of the peoples of underdeveloped areas who may know nothing else about America. In the eighteenth and nine-teenth centuries the United States had thus made good its claim to the role of revolutionary and liberating nation which the U.S.S.R. has sought to play since the Bolshevik revolution of 1917. One might have expected that because of this acknowl-edged historical precedence the colonial peoples would auto-matically turn to the United States for sympathy and under-standing after World War II. Yet this has not usually been the case. What happened to make this promising prospect go awry?

What happened was that the United States, once World War II had ended, suffered a case of arrested anti-colonialism. Until that time America had been urging, in and sometimes out of season, the need for self-government by backward peoples, and had been insisting, often in intemperate tones and on the basis of scanty information, that Britain should give up India, France Indo-China, the Netherlands the Dutch East Indies, and so on. Because of this attitude on our part, the Western colonial pow-ers had come to regard the United States as at least as great a threat to their imperial possessions and authority as the U.S.S.R. Americans, in the view of the British, French, and Dutch spokesmen — among them Professor André Siegfried, noted French historian who is otherwise friendly to the United States — had a disruptive influence on the colonial world.

According to this indictment, Americans gave the natives "ideas" about the possibility of attaining higher standards of living, education, and political independence. They introduced in their own enterprises on colonial territories measures which encouraged native unrest and challenged the authority of colo-nial administrators. And they created the danger that the West-ern powers would ultimately have to surrender their posses-sions in Asia, Africa, and the Middle East, thereby suffering grave losses in terms of economic and strategic advantages which, Western Europeans asserted, were important not only to colonial powers but to the stability of the entire world. It was feared, moreover, that the Americans, who, unlike the Russians, can offer technical facilities and money to colonial peoples, would directly benefit by the liquidation of the Western empires and draw into their own economy the oil, rubber, tin, and other strategic, highly valuable resources which Britain, France, and the Netherlands would be forced to abandon.

For Americans this picture of themselves as revolutionary agitators and potential new exploiters in the colonial world seemed nothing short of fantastic. Yet this was the impression the United States created in Western Europe. The impression was reinforced when the United States in 1936 promised independence to the Philippine Islands by 1946, and then began to cite this decision, faithfully carried out after World War II, as an example to be followed by other colony-owning nations at the earliest possible opportunity. When Lenin, upon taking power in Russia, denounced the Czarist government's unequal treaties with China and Iran, aligned Russia on the side of the colonial peoples, and denounced "imperialist exploitation," it was a great shock for the Western powers, who felt as if a charter member of the colony-holders had suddenly defied the rules and slammed the door on his erstwhile colleagues. But then, it was felt, what could one expect from Bolsheviks? When, however, the United States, which in the West was regarded as a stronghold of capitalism and conservatism, acted with comparable "recklessness" in letting the Philippines go free, some Westerners began to wonder whether Americans were not as radical as the Russians and, being technologically more powerful, would not, in the long run, prove more dangerous to the Western colonial system.

Japan's conquest of Asia in the 1940s dealt an irretrievable blow to the prestige of the white man, already shaken by the Japanese victory over Russia in 1904–1905, and hastened the breakup of colonial empires which had once been ardently advocated by America. World War II completed the erosion of

British rule which had started long before Lenin raised the banner of communism in Asia. By 1945, however, the role of the United States had undergone a drastic change. The young American republic which had sympathized with the aspirations of other peoples in their desire to throw off the colonial yoke, had, without conscious volition on its part, become one of the two greatest powers on the globe and the inheritor of the role once played by the nations of Western Europe.

No sooner did the United States find itself cast in this new role than it began to take on some of the attitudes and even the very state of mind of its predecessors. What had seemed, as late as World War II, legitimate and even welcome ferment on the part of colonial nations suddenly assumed the aspect of a threat to order and stability in highly sensitive strategic areas, from the Suez Canal to Indonesia, from Iran to Indo-China. What had once been greeted here as a promising desire among underdeveloped peoples to achieve independence and to promote social and economic changes began to look like a menacing revolution which would redound to the benefit of Russia and communism. Revolution having by that time become identified in American opinion with communism, any stirring of dissatisfaction with the existing order was apt to be attributed to Communist and/or Russian influence.

Since the colonial areas, by very reason of their backwardness, were peculiarly vulnerable to the promises and pressures of Russia and communism, the main objective of the United States became the maintenance of the existing order of things, lest any change upset the precarious equilibrium and open the floodgates to hostile ideologies, with or without the accompaniment of invading Red armies. The need to "defend" the colonial areas by all possible means to keep them in or bring them into the orbit of the benevolent West as contrasted with the malevolent East, was thought to justify not only economic but also military support of the ruling groups — from Chiang Kai-shek in Formosa to Emperor Bao Dai in Indo-China, from Marshal Pibul Songgram in Thailand to Dr. Syngman Rhee in South Korea. The fact that these men might be distasteful to their own peoples, that they might represent forces and ideas incompatible with avowed American aspirations, and that some of them, notably Marshal Pibul, had not hesitated to cooperate with the Japanese against the West, were brushed aside on the grounds that the end to be attained was the erection of a dam against the communist flood with any materials at hand.

In an attempt to harmonize this policy with our previous anti-colonialism and our postwar defense of democracy against to-talitarianism, the personal dictatorships and feudal authoritarianisms of Egypt and Iran, of Chiang Kai-shek and Bao Dai, were indiscriminately listed as in the camp of "democracies." Nationalist outbursts in the Middle East were described in the American press as "insane," "blind," or "senseless" and their leaders as dangerous "fanatics." And even some of the more responsible American commentators, while urging that the United States enlist Iran and Egypt on the side of the democracies, contended, in querulous tones made familiar by Colonel Blimp, that these countries were not ready either to govern or defend themselves, and that therefore the Western nations would be justified in shouldering the "white man's burden" in areas of particular importance to their interest, notably the oil-producing nations of the Middle East and the Suez Canal. Thus, as the United States found itself forced to assume many of the responsibilities once borne by the British Empire, we began to use double-talk in our discussions of underdeveloped areas. On the one hand, we still spoke of independence, self-government, self-determination, democracy. On the other hand, we argued that relatively weak and unstable nations should be rescued from perdition by the United States, even if this meant postponement or temporary obliteration of independence and subordination of the political and economic aspirations of these nations to the security requirements of the West, regarded as synonymous with the security requirements of the rest of the world.

The result of this dual policy was to maintain in power men and institutions that, without American support, might not have survived the stormy crises of the postwar years. Unpopular rulers, encouraged by American fear of communism, used the threat of unrest among their subjects as a form of genteel blackmail, thereby obtaining aid which helped them to stave off, again and again, the evil hour of undertaking long overdue reforms. Under the circumstances, the United States, in the minds of many Asians, slowly changed from a resplendent Saint George challenging the dragon of colonialism into a staunch supporter of the colonial West and a generous donor of money and arms to feudal overlords who were thus enabled to hold on to power sometimes in defiance of the wishes of their peoples.

This, paradoxically, redounded to the disadvantage of the overlords. For oppression which might have been borne with more or less equanimity as a national burden became intolerable when the native dictators were suspected of being pensioners, and therefore presumably puppets, of the United States. By a transformation that would have seemed fantastic to an earlier generation of Americans, the United States, proponent and inspirer of colonial revolt, became by imperceptible stages and with no direct consultation of the wishes of American voters, the defender of the *status quo* in Asia and other underdeveloped areas. Cheered by this unexpected reprieve, the colonial experts of the Western European nations, listening to newly formulated American arguments against overhasty independence for colonial peoples, could barely refrain from murmuring piously: "We told you so." In a situation where the great power which once fostered revolution could have emerged triumphant, the United States — to the profound relief of the Western colonial nations it had once castigated — appeared to move over to the side of conservatism.

Typical of the complexities of European opinion about American policy toward colonies is a 1951 dispatch of the independent Swiss newspaper, *Neue Züricher Zeitung*, comparable in caliber to the London *Times*. This dispatch from its correspondent in Casablanca, French Morocco, commented on the "anti-colonial" views which President Roosevelt was reported to have expressed to the Sultan of Morocco in 1943 and which, according to the French, inspired the Sultan's subsequent "stiffening" attitude toward France. "But in view of growing American economic interests," the dispatch went on, "Roosevelt's words were also thought, here and there, to indicate a secret intention on the part of the United States to ruin France's position in Morocco in order to be able to step into her shoes." The correspondent then added:

"Objective observers in Morocco are generally convinced, however, that the American actions which are thus criticized proceed from misunderstanding and clumsiness rather than a Machiavellian political design.

"Many Americans, of course, who came to Morocco after the war brought with them something of that missionary spirit which sees in the application of American forms of democracy the ideal solution for the problems of all nations. But on the whole a few months in Morocco have sufficed to make them revise their prejudices. The undeniably impressive achievements of the French in the social, economic, and political fields have been recognized even by convinced opponents of every form of 'colonialism.' And the Americans, for whom the pioneer spirit of the French is particularly striking, cannot understand, and are irritated by, the natives' indolent conservatism and lack of enthusiasm for any kind of modernization."

Torn between its desire to bolster the position of its industrially advanced Western European allies, whose aid it needs to defend Europe, and its long-run urge to advance the welfare of the underdeveloped nations, without whose support it cannot hope to contain Russia and communism in Asia and the Middle East, the United States found itself in a divided state of mind which in an individual similarly situated would be described as schizophrenia. On the one hand, our traditional impulse to help the underdog, to place the technological skills and inventions which made America great at the disposal of the former colonial peoples, continued to animate American policy. The Point Four program — originally described in 1949 as "a bold new program," although it provides only for modest technical aid to underdeveloped areas — was a new attempt to carry on, under altered conditions, the tradition of revolution this country had once symbolized in the colonial world. On the other hand, some Americans uneasily felt that any really bold new program would involve grave dislocations in the colonial economies and, if pressed with vigor and dispatch, would require encroachments on many vested interests whose support seemed at the time essential to defense of the West against Russia and communism. A deep-seated and genuine desire to help other peoples improve their lot was thus pitted against the well-nigh irresistible temptation to let things stay as they were for fear that any change might play into the hands of the Kremlin. All too often fear was allowed to take precedence over reform.

From the outset, moreover, our overwhelming preoccupation with the cold war distorted our plans for technical assistance to underdeveloped areas. For example, the International Development Advisory Committee, headed by Nelson A. Rockefeller, made it clear in its report *Partners in Progress* * that our paramount objective at the present time is to obtain strategic raw materials in Asia and other underdeveloped areas for our own rearmament and that of our allies. Such improvements in native living standards through the reorganization of their

---

* *Partners in Progress,* a report to President Truman by the International Development Advisory Board, foreword by Nelson A. Rockefeller. (Simon and Schuster, New York, 1951.)

primitive economies as does occur would be incidental to this overriding objective of strategic procurement.

Our policy, as outlined in the Rockefeller report, is entirely understandable in terms of the interests of the advanced industrial nations — the United States and its Western European allies. Yet, as seen by the colonial peoples, it is diametrically contrary to their aspirations, and would perpetuate their former colonial status as hewers of wood and drawers of water for the industrialized Western world instead of making them "partners" in their own progress. For the main preoccupation of the backward underdeveloped nations, whether erstwhile colonies or backward areas of Europe and the Middle East, is how to modernize and diversify their economies, hitherto peculiarly dependent on the output of raw materials and foodstuffs whose sharp price fluctuations on world markets condemned these areas to economic instability. Just as the economic development of the less advanced nations, as described in the Rockefeller report, is secondary to the strategic needs of the West; so these strategic needs, from the point of view of the Middle East and Asia, are secondary to their own, too long postponed progress from backward agrarianism to modern economy. Our proclaimed determination to obtain their strategic products, such as oil, rubber, and tin, painfully reminds them of the economic policies followed by the Western colonial powers who, in their opinion, had purposely delayed their economic development in order to hold them in thrall to their authority. These policies, they hoped, would come to an end with the achievement of political independence from British, French, or Dutch rule. To find them revived by the United States, and on grounds formerly invoked by the colonial powers of the West, has in many cases proved a disappointment to the nations of Asia and the Middle East.

To the peoples who had learned to think of the United States as an inspiration in the struggle for freedom, it seemed incred-

ible that Americans should take the side of Britain in Iran and
Egypt and of France in Indo-China and French Morocco. Our
argument that in the great crisis precipitated by the threat of
Russia and communism, the United States, which regards Britain and France as the keystone of the North Atlantic coalition,
could not act in a way that would jeopardize the interests of its
allies in other areas of the globe, carried little conviction to
peoples who are still under colonial rule or have achieved independence only since 1945. In their opinion the United States,
by perpetuating colonialism in any form, is merely defeating
its own ends. Nor are they impressed by American denunciations of communist suppression of human rights in Eastern
Europe or China, pointing to the repression of native political
opponents by France, for instance, in Tunisia and Morocco,
without notable protest on our part. They recognize that we
are genuinely trying to improve conditions in South Korea and
that we urge the French to grant self-government in Indo-
China, but they regard these measures as falling short of the
vigorous policy of support for the colonial peoples they had
expected the United States to follow.

Because of the vast differences between our respective points
of departure and arrival in history, many things which we, in
all honesty, regard as right and desirable, the nations of Asia
and the Middle East, also in all honesty, regard as wrong and
undesirable. The Asians do not want to hear constantly about
our great wealth and our amazing ingenuity, which make them
uneasy about their poverty and backwardness. They do not
want to be recipients of our charity, no matter how generous.
They do not want the Western powers to protect them with
military force against Russia and communism if this means the
perpetuation of governments which they oppose and which,
in their opinion, represent a stumbling block to reform, or if
our military intervention spells a general Asian war, which
would ruin the newly independent nations. They do not want

institutions that masquerade as democracy established under the protection of Western military and financial aid, while behind the ramshackle Westernized façade native rulers continue to oppress the masses and encourage black-market operations. They do not want to receive either as gifts or as loans they will have to repay, machinery so complex that their illiterate and technically unskilled people will not be able to operate it. They do not want us to talk only to a handful of their top people and neglect the workers and peasants.

Conditions in one country can never be entirely duplicated in another. It is wholly unrealistic to assume that the fortunate combination of natural resources, historical circumstances, and special skills which have contributed in such remarkable degree to the development of American society are not unique, and could be repeated, with relative ease, in nations vastly different from the United States in their history, traditions, and economic resources. The belief that the American system can be transported, as on a magic carpet, to other lands and climes with hardly a sea change creates false illusions here, the subsequent nonfulfillment of which then fosters suspicions about the efficiency and reliability of foreign governments. It also creates dangerous illusions among the peoples abroad when we encourage them to build a dreamworld on the basis of blueprints drawn up to our particular specifications.

It is certainly a praiseworthy objective to arouse a spirit of hopefulness on the part of peoples until now bereft of hope, and to encourage them to expect that, with the determined application of scientific knowledge plus managerial and technical experience, even human beings now judged backward by Western standards can look forward to marked improvement of their lot. But to focus the attention of the countries receiving our aid on the admirable achievements of the United States and directly or indirectly suggest that they might in the visible future come to emulate our achievements is to write out promissory notes which we may find it difficult to honor upon presentation. What if these nations lack the combination of coal, oil, and iron necessary to create heavy modern industry, as may prove true of India and, to a lesser extent, China, not to speak of nations hitherto dependent on the output of one or two foodstuffs or raw materials, such as Iran with oil, Chile with copper and nitrates, Bolivia with tin? What if they have hitherto been urged by the colonial powers — and also in the case of the Philippines by the United States before the islands achieved independence in 1946 — to concentrate their efforts on the production of a few food crops or strategic minerals, chiefly for export, and have had no opportunity to retain sufficient quantities of their products for the development and modernization of their own economy, even on a modest scale? What, as is true in many areas of the globe, if climatic conditions are unfavorable to the kind of prolonged physical exertion which has characterized the economic development of the United States and Western Europe?

Can we, in all honesty, undertake to provide substitute resources and alternative climate so as to equalize the conditions of other nations with our own? Shall we reduce our living standards to the level of less fortunate lands? Or must we scale down our expectations of what can be done in Asia, and learn to help other peoples to improve their conditions not in the frame of reference familiar to us but in the frame of reference set by their particular circumstances? Can we force Western colonial administrators or native feudal rulers of underdeveloped areas and seemingly slothful populations to abandon their customary practices and conform to our far more vigorous and, by their standards, unorthodox methods? Or would such an approach be tantamount to a social revolution which we would hesitate to launch for fear of the effect it might have on the established order?

Could we coerce native labor to work longer hours at a

greater rate of exertion, or should we let them proceed at their own pace, unsatisfactory as it might seem to us, for fear of being accused of resorting to forced labor? Is it desirable for us to carry our political, economic, and social ideas into underdeveloped lands — as our missionaries once did for the propagation of Christianity — or will these ideas merely disrupt, as Christian missionary teachings often did, the existing structure of ancient or weary societies without substituting viable alternatives? Can America, in short, expect unquestioning compliance with our standards and policies and uniformity of thought and action as the guerdon of our aid?

What, then, do the underdeveloped nations want, and what can we do to help them satisfy their wants? Arthur Goodfriend, in his graphic book, *The Only War We Seek,** has vividly answered these questions in pictures and a few pungent phrases. They want us to understand, as they do, that they are still one hundred years or more behind Western Europe and the United States, and are filled with a passionate desire to catch up with our economic development. They want to learn short cuts, so that they need not spend a century or more arriving at the point where we are today — a point from which we will presumably have advanced far a century hence. They want simple tools and machinery that their people can learn to use in a short time. They have learned, through harsh experience, that political independence and parliamentary institutions do not bring about the economic and social millennium. They want advice from Americans and other Westerners who are not conscious of color bars, who are genuinely interested in getting to the "rice-roots" level of Asian nations, who will be sufficiently generous to see and applaud what is good in the civilizations of nations other than their own, who will not show contempt for less technologically advanced peoples. They want to develop

* Published for Americans for Democratic Action by Farrar, Strauss and Young, New York, 1951.

a modern way of life fitted to their own particular needs, not to accept a ready-made carbon copy of the American way of life.

They want to help themselves, and welcome our help in this task, provided we do not offer it either as charity, which would offend their dignity, or as payment for their political and military support, which would offend their ardent desire for independence. They want aid which will not be so far beyond their financial means as to transform them once more into pensioners, or puppets, or wards, or hirelings of the Western nations. They want aid which will not be offered from on high by the United States and other Western nations through administrators who will tell the "natives" what to do and not to do. They want to be genuine "partners" of the West in the transformation of the world, participating jointly and on a basis of equality in all efforts undertaken to improve agriculture, consumer industries, health, literacy, housing, land ownership, and so on.

They realize, sometimes with an acuteness so painful that it incites them to what we regard as unreasonable acts of violence against the West, the vast extent of their poverty, their technical backwardness, their inadequacy to deal with the complex problems of modern life as compared with our wealth and technological "know-how." But they think that the very vastness of their difficulties should inspire the United States not to hold them back for fear of communist gains, but to spur them forward, so as to hasten the moment when they can govern, sustain, and defend their populations more effectively than they do today.

How can the United States meet this challenge in Asia and the Middle East and, tomorrow, in Africa? We can do so only if we approach the underdeveloped countries in a spirit of humility, ready not only to teach them but also to learn from them. We cannot intervene by force. But we can offer the best there is in us as a possible example.

7

THE CHALLENGE
IN EUROPE

Assuming, as is done throughout this book, that hot war
with Russia does not occur in Europe, the continuation
of the present "no war, no peace" situation will present the
United States with three major questions: (1) how can our
allies in Western Europe be integrated into a larger political
and economic unit, and what unit should it be? (2) how can the
obstacles to greater productivity within the Western European
nations be removed so that the population as a whole can share
in the benefits promised by modern industry and modern
science? and (3) how can we prevent the various conflicts in
Western Europe, which fear of Russia and communism have
hitherto held in check, from creating fissures in the North
Atlantic Treaty coalition?

The challenge of these three questions to our imagination
and patience is often obscured by three current American assumptions. The first of these is that the entire European continent is fashioned of the same cloth and cut to the same pattern,
and that if only Russia would withdraw to its own borders
Europe would achieve political and economic unity on the
model of the United States, free of frontiers and of barriers
to trade and population movements. The second assumption
is that the economic and social system of Western Europe is

similar to ours, and that therefore any European criticism of this system or any attempt to alter it in the direction of a more controlled economy represents a criticism of the American system and must be feared as an entering wedge for socialism in the United States. The third assumption is that the only problems confronting Western Europe are created by Russia and communism.

The facts, as we have been gradually discovering in the postwar years, are far different from these assumptions. Europe is made up of national states whose peoples struggled for centuries to attain internal cohesion and freedom from external pressures. Nor is the day of nationalism yet over, as some had expected it would be after World War II. On the contrary, the totalitarian ideologies of nazism, fascism, and communism, far from overriding national sentiment, actually raised it to the nth degree. The perils of both foreign conquest and civil strife during the past twenty years intensified the national desire for survival even in countries that had seemed to have outgrown the more flamboyant era of nationalism, like the Low Countries and the Scandinavian nations.

Meanwhile, in Eastern Europe, where the achievements of national independence had been held back by the oppression of the multinational empires of Kaiser Germany, Czarist Russia, and imperial Austria-Hungary, new nations emerged after 1919, encouraged by Woodrow Wilson's doctrine of "self-determination." The intoxication of their new nationalism made subordination to any supranational authority even less appealing than it was for the older, more settled national states of Western Europe. Yet the multiplying crises of the interwar period clearly revealed that small and weak nations do not have the capacity to resist the encroachments — political, economic, and ideological — of powerful neighbors, and over the long run can find no political stability or economic security except through membership in some larger group.

But what group will it be? The Eastern European nations which during the interwar years tried to form regional groups, confessed discouragement with plans for a Danubian federation or a Balkan bloc, and their exiled leaders now favor a United States of Europe bringing together East and West. Since 1947 Americans have strongly urged a regional union of Western Europe, asserting: "Europe must unite or perish," and contending that a united Europe of the West could achieve the prosperity of the United States. But not only have Americans minimized the thousand and one difficulties of uniting the countries of Western Europe, forgetting the trials and tribulations experienced by the American colonies under far easier circumstances; not only have they drawn altogether too facile comparisons between the historical development of Europe and America, which cannot stand the test of dispassionate examination, Americans have also failed to take into account that one of the greatest assets of the United States is its unique combination of industrial and agricultural resources, which has made it possible for us to build here a well-balanced and relatively self-sufficient economy. This would not be true of a Western European union. Most of the nations of that area are highly industrialized — Britain, West Germany, Belgium, France, the Netherlands, Norway, Sweden, Northern Italy — and compete with each other for markets; and only two — France and Denmark — can provide adequate food for their population or export foodstuffs, while the majority, notably Britain, West Germany, and Italy, urgently depend on food imports for survival. A Western European economic union would be a union of Pittsburghs, Detroits, and Clevelands without the agricultural hinterland provided here by Iowa, Kansas, and Nebraska.

Not only are the economics of a Western European union difficult, but so are its politics. For the time being, Britain, whether ruled by Conservatives or Laborites, holds its ties with the Commonwealth and the Empire in higher regard than the potential union it might effect with the nations of continental Europe whose relatively unstable governments, particularly in France, the British view with a jaundiced eye. And unless Britain is a full member of the Western European union, accepts the Schuman plan for the pooling of coal and steel, and incorporates its armed forces in the European army proposed by the French to avoid the revival of an independent German army, France will continue to feel that such a union will be dangerously lopsided, for sooner or later it would come to be dominated by Germany.

From the point of view of the French, who do not yet believe in the regeneration of the Germans, the possibility of a viable Western European union without British participation would arise only if the German nation remains permanently divided into West and East states. For then West Germany, with a population of 45 to 50 million, would be in rough balance with the populations of France and Italy, averaging over 40 million each. But if German nationalist sentiment triumphs over the artificial obstacles of Allied dissensions, as sooner or later it is bound to do, and the Germans achieve national unity, 70 million Germans would prove, in the eyes of France and of other Western nations which have not forgotten the ravages of nazi conquest, so overwhelming a force as to transform the proposed union into a domain of the newly restored *Reich*. The same would be true of the Schuman plan and of the European army which, under such circumstances, could become instruments of and not safeguards against the revival of militant Germanism.

The Schuman Plan Assembly created in August 1952, in which six countries — West Germany, France, Italy, the Netherlands, Luxembourg, and Belgium are represented — took an important step toward political unification when it decided to draft plans for a Western European union. Britain, however, promptly expressed its fear that an economically revived Germany, rearmed for participation in the European Defense Community, would dominate such a union. At the same time Britain made it clear that while it was ready to cooperate with the Schuman Plan Assembly, it had no intention of subordinating its ties with the Commonwealth to participation in a Western European union.

The Schuman-plan countries, for their part, have no illusions about the problems that face them in their task of unification. They realize that Western Europe cannot hope to create an economically self-sufficient region, and will have to look to Africa and, if possible, Asia and the Middle East for raw materials, and to the United States for investment capital. Nor are they irrevocably opposed to considering the possibility of trade in nonstrategic goods with Russia and Eastern Europe. Their leaders, moreover, continue to hope that some day the Eastern European nations, free of Russia's control, will participate in a United States of Europe. All discussions of a Western European union, therefore, show a high degree of fluidity, with some plans shading off toward an Atlantic union with the United States and Canada, and others toward union between Eastern and Western Europe, but never overlooking stronger economic ties between the Western European nations and the remnants of their colonial empires in Africa. In spite of this fluidity, many thoughtful Europeans are convinced that belief in the possibility of a united Europe has an invigorating psychological effect on their peoples; and especially on the young who are tired of hearing about wars and conflicts and would welcome genuine European cooperation. Therefore, they feel, it is essential to keep this idea alive, even if it cannot be given political embodiment in the immediate future. And meanwhile they hope — this is particularly true of the French — that a Western European union will restrain West Germany from resuming its career of aggression and provide a counterbalance to the two extra-European superpowers, the United States and the U.S.S.R. Western European union is thus expected to act as a solvent for some of the most arduous problems that have haunted Europe for centuries. But if it is to succeed, it must be the result of Western Europe's own efforts, not an artificial structure erected to meet the requirements or specifications of the United States.

If we had the advantage of living in an ideal world — which, obviously, it is not our privilege to do — the most natural form of European union would be a union of Western and Eastern Europe, with Britain in the West and Russia in the East remaining on the side lines as interested but not malevolent observers willing to cooperate but not to interfere or dominate. For then the industrial resources of the Western European nations could be busily employed in developing the still relatively underdeveloped areas of Eastern Europe and the Balkans and in raising their living standards, while these areas, in turn, through intensified development of their agricultural and raw-material resources, could provide Western Europe with at least some of the foods and raw materials, notably coal, which it must currently import from the United States and other overseas countries.

There is no doubt that, in an ideal world, the Eastern European nations, even if they remained, like Yugoslavia, under communist regimes, would welcome the opportunity to trade with Western Europe. At the present time, however, it seems unlikely that the U.S.S.R. will abandon its economic control of Eastern Europe, which supplies food, raw materials, and some manufactured goods — the latter primarily coming from the one industrialized nation of the area, Czechoslovakia — to the vast Russian economy, unless it, in turn, can find safe alternative sources of supply. Nor is the United States for the time being willing to permit the Western European nations, no matter how hard pressed they may be for dollars, to trade on any large scale with Eastern Europe, for fear that their industrial exports would reinforce the military potential of the U.S.S.R.

Ultimately, however, unless another world war occurs, it is difficult to see how the United States can indefinitely keep the Western European nations — particularly Britain and Germany, which are already engaged in fierce competition with each other, as well as with a revived Japan, for export markets — from trading with Eastern Europe and Russia, particularly if the Kremlin, as it is already doing, holds out to Western European manufacturers the prospect of an outlet in China. The only possible alternative to this future Russian-controlled outlet would be an electrifying decision by the United States to provide here a far larger market for Western European exports than has so far been contemplated by most Americans — or even free trade as proposed by Henry Ford.

Such an effort on our part would have to recognize squarely that an economic union of the Atlantic nations, composed of the United States, Canada, and the countries of Western Europe, would offer the only practicable alternative to restoration of an undivided European continent. This would mean that instead of merely urging the Europeans to knock down their frontier posts and abandon their tariff and immigration barriers, we ourselves would offer to open our market and throw wide our gates to untrammeled traffic of both men and goods within the confines of the Atlantic community. Such a step would certainly challenge Russia's influence in Europe. It would put new heart into Europeans who want to break out of the narrow confines of nationalism but have not been sure where they could go once they had made the break. And it would stir the imagination of the young generation in Europe and elsewhere, less tied down than their elders to the traditions of nationalism. But it would constitute a revolutionary move for our own nationalists, who have hitherto held fast to the concept of national sovereignty and have regarded even modest adjustments to the trade and immigration problems of other nations as a threat to the interests of the United States. When we urge our friends in Western Europe to take the plunge and accept regional economic union, we might bear in mind that this kind of cooperation, like charity, could well begin at home.

If, however, we prefer not to disturb our own industrial and agricultural producers, both employers and labor, by increasing our imports from Western Europe, we might decide to offer a permanent subsidy to that area — not as a gift but as a form of investment for our self-protection. This is what Paul G. Hoffman, former director of the Economic Cooperation Administration and president of the Ford Foundation, proposed in a speech at the *New York Herald Tribune* forum in October 1951, when he said it would be to the advantage of the United States to set aside about one per cent of the annual national income for outright grants — not repayable loans but nonrepayable grants — to the nations of Western Europe.

This proposal, generous in intent, raises three main questions. First, and most obviously, it would have as its aim, if not as its result, an artificial diversion, dictated by the current cold war against Russia, of Western European manufactured goods from the areas where they could be of immediate and far-reaching benefit, notably Eastern Europe, the Balkans, Russia itself, and communist China. Desirable as such a diversion may seem temporarily on political and strategic grounds, it is doubtful that it would over the long run prove beneficial to the welfare of the international community as a whole. Second, an American subsidy of Western Europe — for such it would be — might have the dangerous effect of all charity operations. It might weaken the fiber of self-reliance and self-help among the Europeans, who would get used to a permanent handout from the United States. Then, if we should find it necessary, for one domestic reason or another, to suspend or abandon the subsidy, the United States would become subject to abuse by nations which would feel that their economies had been undermined by our withdrawal. (It would be particularly ironic if American businessmen who had vigorously opposed such projects as the WPA in the United States during the 1930s should favor a comparable program for Western Europe.) And, third, it is difficult to see how a subsidy could be granted by the United States in perpetuity without bringing here a demand for some form of American intervention in the political affairs of the recipient nations. Should this occur, opposition to political intervention by the United States would become a popular rallying point for European national leaders seeking to achieve power, and our aid to Western Europe might paradoxically reinforce nationalism instead of alleviating it, just as British intervention in the affairs of the Middle East countries has fanned latent nationalism into a reckless and potentially destructive force. In 1952 the Western European nations were making it clear that they wanted to end their postwar dependence on the United States. "Trade, not aid," the slogan of Richard A. Butler, Chancellor of the Exchequer in Winston Churchill's Cabinet, was winning adherents throughout Western Europe.

But whatever course the United States decides to pursue with respect to the problem of unity in Western Europe, we shall also have to realize that the existing economic system in many of the countries of that region is not, as some Americans believe, a facsimile of the American system. Far from it. Until the end of World War II, when the ferment generated by nazi conquest, communist propaganda, and national resistance movements flowed over into postwar demands for economic and social reforms, most of Western Europe had an economic system which, for lack of a better label, continued to be described as capitalism. The use of this term, which we also apply to our economic system, caused many of us to believe that the Western European nations were in all aspects of production similar to the United States.

It is only as a result of the multiplying contacts developed between the United States and Europe since 1947, largely through the efforts of the Economic Cooperation Administration, that our business and labor leaders have begun to see the profound fundamental differences between the economy of most of the Western European nations and our own. Now we have started to realize, but without as yet overcoming the time lag in our understanding of Western European conditions, that while the economy of the United States continued to develop apace into the twentieth century, and is still in a state of "permanent revolution," that of Western Europe stopped changing sometime in the nineteenth century. Consequently, compared to our own relatively flexible and highly experimental economy, marked by social mobility, fresh inventiveness, adaptation to changing circumstances, and willingness as well as capacity to distribute the benefits of increased productivity among the population as a whole, Western European economy had been living in a strait jacket of production cartels, labor restrictions, social rigidities, reluctance to consider new inventions or adapt to new world conditions, lack of concern on the part of the minority who are wealthy for the needs and aspirations of the majority who are poor, and either incapacity or unwillingness to translate improved productivity into higher wages for workers and lower prices on more consumer goods for the public in general.

It is these rigidities and inequalities, which neither Europe's business leaders nor its politicians seemed capable or willing to correct, far more than ideological attachment to any given doctrine, which made popular acceptance of socialism and nationalization seem not only desirable but also necessary in Western Europe. The transition from cartelized, monopolistic private enterprise, which kept prices high and wages as well as output of consumer goods low, to nationalized government-administered enterprises seemed a step forward to people who hoped that the governments would at least bring about greater equality in the distribution of available products or, as the

British put it, "fair shares for all." If we assume that people
like the British, the Norwegians, or the Swedes, with their
deeply ingrained attachment to political freedom, turned to
socialism because they had despaired of political democracy,
had chosen totalitarianism and were striving to create a society
on the model of George Orwell's *1984*, then we shall completely misunderstand the process of economic and social
change which Britain and the Scandinavian countries have
undergone in the past quarter century. Nor shall we see that the
invulnerability of the British and Scandinavians to the tempta-
tions of communism has been a direct result of the new hope
they have seen in the possibilities of socialism. This invulnerability is in strong contrast to the situation in France, Italy, and
West Germany, which have not yet come to grips, or have done
so only halfheartedly, with the problems of altering the process
of production in such a way as to benefit the masses — not only
a luxury-enjoying minority indifferent to social responsibilities,
— and where either communism or neo-nazism and neo-fascism
retain a strong hold on the workers, the peasants, and the poorer
middle class.

Since 1945 the peoples of Western Europe have learned, by
harsh experience, that nationalization does not of itself bring
about a rise in production and a consequent improvement in
living standards, and that socialism does not automatically spell
the millennium. But they do not see how a return to presocialist
capitalism will effect the social equalization which they regard
as a prerequisite of twentieth-century democracy; and they fear
that adoption of the American pattern which Paul Hoffman
described as "painful competition" would, under European
circumstances, merely widen the already vast gap between the
few who live in luxury and the many who, even in the periods
of relative prosperity, are barred from educational, economic,
and social opportunities to improve their lot and that of their
children.

The idea of the "welfare state" has come to stay in Western Europe, and we must expect to see it maintained by all political leaders, irrespective of ideology, whether Aneurin Bevan or Winston Churchill, whether Premier Antoine Pinay, conservative small industrialist, or General de Gaulle. No government in Western Europe would want to take the risk of permitting living standards to deteriorate to the point where the workers, in desperation, might turn to one form of extremism or another, whether communism or a new form of nazism or fascism. Because of the precariousness of the European economies, still in a state of convalescence, the danger of internal upheaval looms much larger in the minds of governments in Western Europe than the danger of Russian aggression or even of Communist propaganda and infiltration.

Our failure during the early postwar years to understand the economic and social differences between the United States and Western Europe has been a constant source of astonishment to our European friends. Do Americans, they ask, really want to salvage in Europe a small group of industrialists who are intent on maintaining monopolies bolstered by cartels; who are more anxious to keep prices high through restricted production than they are to make consumer goods available to ever larger sections of the population by lowering prices through increased productivity; who have little or no concern for the social welfare of factory workers and still resist labor participation in the political and economic life of their countries; who often make a blatant display of their wealth, notably in West Germany and Italy, without a thought for the unfavorable impression this may create among the masses, still subsisting on living standards we would regard as shockingly low compared to our own?

Or, our friends ask, is it possible that those Americans who have opposed economic and social changes in the United States, have fought labor unions tooth and nail, have denounced all measures that might be regarded as contributing to the development of the "welfare state," who see in any demand for reform dangerous signs of "radicalism" — is it possible that those Americans, having been repeatedly defeated on the home front, are still carrying on abroad the battle against the institutions and practices they abhor here, in the hope that by bolstering them in France or Italy, in Spain or Formosa they might eventually introduce them in the United States?

But if this is the case, then, our friends ask, how does it happen that a Democratic administration in Washington committed to a program for broadening economic and social rights and opportunities often appeared to practice, as if it were its own, a policy which had been identified abroad as that of its political opponents? Had acquiescence in the *status quo* abroad been the price paid for bipartisan foreign policy? Or had the Truman Administration itself failed to discern the fundamental contradiction in its position, when it urged other countries to transform themselves in the image of the United States, yet hoped this transformation would be effected by governments fearful of change with as little disturbance of the existing order as possible?

The Soviet leaders and, echoing them, Communists everywhere continue to believe that no contradiction exists, that the United States is a nation by nature irrevocably opposed to all improvements in the lot of its workers and farmers whose government, even if it were well-intentioned, could do nothing in the direction of reform because it is a prisoner of Wall Street, and that therefore no one should be surprised to find the United States applying abroad the reactionary policy it pursues at home. But our friends in Europe who have seen with their own eyes our great economic and social revolution of the thirties and forties are not taken in by communist propaganda. They know that Americans understand the need for change, that we are not wedded to reaction and economic and social stratification. If, however, through misguided policy, the United States becomes identified with what the Europeans regard as obsolete institutions, reactionary leaders, and inadequate production, then the Communists will have an easy task convincing the dissatisfied and disillusioned that, had it not been for American aid, the objectionable institutions, leaders, and practices would have collapsed and disappeared long ago for lack of native support. If, on the contrary, the United States makes an earnest effort to understand the interests, needs, and aspirations of the masses of the population — not merely the minority of businessmen, bankers, government officials, landowners, and diplomats at the top — and helps to meet these needs and fulfill these aspirations, then it may not win unstinted praise, but it will at least have the satisfaction of seeing the ideals it has been preaching abroad translated into reality.

The painful fact must be faced that the mere giving of American economic and technical assistance to the nations of Europe, no matter how generous or prolonged, will not of itself alter existing conditions or build a sound basis for future improvements unless it is channeled through modernized political, economic, and social institutions. Otherwise our assistance will ultimately prove as sterile as water poured upon sand. It will not be properly absorbed; it will not fructify the recipient. It will merely perpetuate the existing order and postpone the difficult hour of change, thereby ensuring that change, when it does come, will not be peaceful and gradual — as it has proved in this country — but sudden and violent.

We must constantly be on the watch for the possibility that our aid to Europe may merely consolidate existing economic inequalities. Two aspects of this problem have already become clearly apparent. Because of our official diffidence about working closely with labor groups and with Socialist parties, our representatives abroad usually tend to limit their personal contacts to the minority of those who have wealth and authority.

They hesitate to take any measures which might weaken the property or power position of this minority, even if such measures may ultimately be in the national interest of the United States. Thus the Department of State and, to a lesser extent, the more outspoken Economic Cooperation Administration, have acted in a gingerly manner when it came to suggesting that, if a given country were to continue to receive American aid, the local government should insist on the payment of taxes by the wealthy industrialists and landowners who often, instead of aiding their own national economy, send their funds for safekeeping to Switzerland or the United States. The result has been that, while millions of Americans with relatively modest incomes pay taxes, a portion of which goes into foreign aid expenditures, the rich of France and Italy and Greece find it possible to perpetuate luxurious living standards and to develop no sense of responsibility for the difficulties of their own less fortunate fellow citizens. For they confidently expect that, as long as the threat of communism can be invoked, the United States will continue to bail them out.

The second aspect of this situation is that our aid tends to remain on the top levels of a recipient country's economy and often does not percolate to the factory workers in the form of higher wages and greater availability of reasonably priced consumer goods. By a curious paradox, our powerful economy which has been profoundly mellowed in the past quarter of a century by a growing sense of social responsibility pours its resources into other countries with the admirable avowed purpose of raising the living standards of their masses; yet it often succeeds only in maintaining the living standards of a minority with a long tradition of special privilege. Nor will supranational measures like the Schuman Plan alter this situation unless reforms are made from the bottom up.

It is of paramount importance for future understanding between the United States and the democratic elements of

Western Europe that we should dispel the anxiety these elements often feel lest we use our economic power to impede changes many Europeans regard as essential. This anxiety was expressed in 1951 by a reviewer in the liberal, anti-communist *Manchester Guardian* who, commenting on the little book, *Peace Can Be Won,* by Paul G. Hoffman, advocate of "socially conscious capitalism" for Europe, said: "No doubt he could develop this soundly. It would have to be clear, however, that Socialist countries are not expected to turn their clocks back or even to retard them."

How can we arrive at an intelligible contact with the masses of the population in Europe? How can we learn to talk to them in a language they understand, as the Communists seemingly have learned to do? One of the most effective methods, which we have only recently adopted, is to send abroad not only professional diplomats and businessmen, but also representatives of our labor unions and farm organizations. These men, although accustomed to conditions here usually far in advance of those faced by the European masses, are at least more apt to have a sympathetic understanding of their problems than our diplomatic or military spokesmen. But even here a warning is in order. For American labor and farm representatives, in turn, must not limit their activities to the top leaders of comparable organizations in Europe, who themselves may be out of touch with sentiment among the rank and file of their followers; they must take the time to become acquainted with the needs and desires of the average worker and farmer, to which the Communists pay continuous and vigilant attention.

The mere fact, however, of showing to Europe that our labor unions are no longer regarded here as a threat to free enterprise, or relegated to the periphery of American political life, in itself has a significant impact on European opinion, which had come to believe that the United States is ruled by powerful industrial and financial interests inimical to labor. If we are to present our labor unions in this enlarged role abroad, we may find it necessary to assure them also a larger role at home in the formulation of policy, both domestic and foreign. For it would obviously be impossible, over the long run, to expect that American labor will act merely as a mouthpiece for policies it does not help to fashion. Thus while sharing with the Europeans our technical knowledge of how to raise their industrial and agricultural sights and effect social changes through increased productivity, we may find that we are learning from them how to bring about political transformations through increased participation by labor in this country's domestic and foreign policies.

Both well-informed businessmen and well-informed labor leaders in the United States have become increasingly aware that it is not in consonance with the facts to compare businessmen and labor conditions in Europe with those in the United States, and they have been as critical of obsolete employer-worker relations on the Continent as spokesmen for Europe's Labor and Socialist parties. At the second Congress of the anti-communist International Confederation of Free Trade Unions (ICFTU) in Milan in 1951, when Europeans denounced capitalists in general, representatives of American labor declared that capitalism in Europe and capitalism in the United States are evidently two quite different things. American workers, they said, have no affection for European monopolies which produce little, charge high prices, and dodge taxes.

By contrast, they contended, American capitalists, with their mass production, their constant reinvestment in new equipment, with the relatively low prices of their products, and their substantial tax payments — not to speak of their voluntary contributions to charitable and civic undertakings in which they actively participate — have helped to give American workers the highest living standard in the world. Under our system, said American labor representatives, the unions prefer to demand good wages and good working conditions and leave the operation of business to management — in sharp contrast to the policy of the West German labor unions and Social Democrats who in 1951 insisted on and won the right for labor participation in the management of some industrial enterprises on a basis of equality with employers.

At the same time thoughtful leaders of American labor like Irving Brown, permanent representative of the American Federation of Labor in Europe, pointed out that American unions have had an entirely different history from those of Europe. American unions, he noted, never had to overthrow the remnants of feudalism, as was the case on the European continent. Developing in a society where the equality of man had been long imbedded in constitutional practices, they were not under the necessity, as was true of Europe's leaders, to fight for political democracy before they could win economic and social improvements.

The problems of Europe's economy, so far as the past is concerned, were not of our making. Nor can it be said that they were created in the first instance by Russia. The Kremlin and local Communists have taken advantage of these problems by applying various pressures on Western Europe, while we, for our part, have sought to alleviate them with Marshall Plan and Mutual Security Program aid. But the Western European nations themselves will have to tackle these problems if long-term alleviation is to be found for recurring crises, if future American aid is to be constructively used, and if communism is to be permanently defeated.

Similarly, the political problems of Europe were not, in the first instance, created by the United States and, in important respects, they present problems also for Russia. The central fact that Germany is the most highly industrialized nation on the Continent with a 70-million population highly trained in modern industrial skills and possessing aggressive energy cannot be changed by any amount of diplomatic prestidigitation. This powerful nation, which in World War II succeeded in conquering practically the whole continent, in gravely menacing Britain, and in severely mauling Russia, will continue to trouble its neighbors for many years to come unless it can demonstrate that it has forsworn the ways of militarism and, like France after the Napoleonic wars, has settled down to peaceful cooperation with weaker nations. Until this has been demonstrated, Russia and Eastern Europe, as well as France, will continue to fear Germany and to take whatever safeguards seem to them most adequate against the possibly harmful results of German rearmament. If the United States should decide to foster the "liberation" of Russia's satellites in Eastern Europe, it would have to bear in mind their legitimate anxiety about the restoration of Germany's military might, and give them some concrete assurance against another *Drang nach Osten.* And if ultimately this country should, from "situations of strength," proceed to negotiate with Russia, one of the major items the United States would have to consider is the kind of military balance that can be struck in Eastern Europe so that the Russians will no longer have a legitimate fear of another 1914 or 1941, of new German threats to Moscow and Stalingrad.

The challenge that faces us in Europe is thus far more complex than a program of temporary aid to war-stricken countries and of a military alliance to contain Russia. We must find ways of helping Western Europeans carry out, within the framework of political democracy, the Second Industrial Revolution they need in order to adapt their economies to the conditions of the twentieth century. If we do not do it, the Communists — or some new brand of Nazis or Fascists — will do it instead. For the task cries out to be done. Perpetuation of the existing shackled capitalist institutions in Europe, it is now increasingly realized here, not only weakens the joint defense efforts of the North Atlantic coalition but serves the interests of commu-

nism. The best safeguard against communist influence and the
strongest bulwark of the West is the growth, with our aid but
not at our direction, of a responsible and technologically well-
equipped mixed economy combining intelligent and really en-
terprising private enterprise with some undertakings which
are either directed by the government or in which the government plays an important part. We must also do our best to
understand that great as is the present fear of Russia in Western
Europe, any decline in its influence which our aid may help to
ensure will bring back into the foreground the unresolved
problems of Germany's dominant position in Europe, of Britain's abstention from participation in Western European union,
and the various controversial questions which the cold war
has kept on ice, such as the Saar, Trieste, and the future of
the Oder-Neisse territories taken from Germany by Russia and
Poland in 1945.

Even in the most unlikely case that Russia withdraws into
its 1939 borders, Europe will still face many conflicts and controversies. It therefore remains essential, if we are to formulate
a long-term program of foreign policy, that we deploy more
energy than in the past to understand political and economic
conditions in Europe and to hear with sympathy the point of
view of Europeans which on many points, for historically understandable reasons, is different from ours. Comprehension on
our part of what Europe thinks will bring about a closer relationship between us and our Western allies than either formal
treaty arrangements or reams of costly propaganda about the
advantages of our way of life. The same thing is true of the
far different problems we face in Asia and other underdeveloped areas of the world.

8

THE CHALLENGE
IN ASIA

Assuming, again, that a large-scale war with Russia does not occur in Asia, the continuation of the present "no war, no peace" situation will present the United States with three major questions: (1) how can we help the Asian peoples achieve economic as well as political stability without imposing on them the American way of life and, at the same time, preserve them from using methods of dictatorship and forced labor which communist leaders have instituted in Russia and China? (2) how can we help to strike a balance of forces in Asia which would simultaneously satisfy the need of the United States, Australia, and New Zealand for security, of Britain and Japan for markets and raw materials, and of China and Russia for safeguards against the revival of a militant Japan? and (3) how can we eradicate as swiftly as possible the psychological tensions created by memories of the white man's condescension toward nonwhite peoples — a condescension which is not yet entirely a thing of the past?

Unlike the long-industrialized nations of Western Europe, the Asian nations must in a short period of time overcome a great lag in their industrial and agricultural development, their living standards, their political experience. The nations of Asia have no desire for totalitarianism on the Russian model. But neither are they prepared to wait fifty or a hundred years in the hope that by gradual stages they may emerge from their present politically feudal, economically underdeveloped condition, and achieve some of the good things of life promised to them by modern science as interpreted by American technicians. Nor can we expect a warm welcome in Asia and the Middle East if, on the plea of protecting the countries of this region from Russia and communism, we give the slightest indication that we may reintroduce the colonial practices of Britain, France, and the Netherlands or even show sympathy for these practices.

If we are to establish satisfactory working relationships with the peoples of Asia and the Middle East, we must, first of all, convince them that Washington is not irrevocably committed to following the policies developed over past centuries by the Western colonial powers but, instead, will use its judgment independently on each issue as it arises. Such a demonstration of independence on our part will inevitably cause heartburning in Britain and France. These countries, not unnaturally, feel that the United States, a newcomer in colonial matters, is taking advantage of their weakened condition to reap the benefits of trade and political prestige while for the most part escaping the obligations and onus of "the white man's burden."

That conflicts still exist between the interests of the Western colonial powers and their current or erstwhile colonial subjects is made evident by every day's headlines. In weighing these conflicting interests, American officials will have to decide which is the lesser of the two dangers: to offend the sensitivities of the Western European nations, or to antagonize the underdeveloped areas and thereby, perhaps, lose them to the influence of Russia. Shall we reestablish Britain in the Middle East as "executive agent" of the free West, as suggested by Geoffrey Crowther, editor of the liberal London *Economist*, and risk inheriting the hostility which the peoples of this area, rightly or wrongly, have developed for Britain? Or shall we ourselves assume responsibility for the defense and development of areas now or formerly controlled by Britain, France, and the Netherlands, with or without the blessing of the United Nations?

The decision in each case must depend on the over-all estimate we make of the major forces shaping events in Asia and the Middle East. If we believe that temporizing action which must postpone economic, as well as political, independence for some underdeveloped areas, will at the same time build a safe retaining wall against Russia and communism, we may think we are justified in supporting the control of Britain and France over what is left of their colonies, even though this may alienate the colonial peoples as well as the newly independent nations such as India, Pakistan, and Indonesia.

If, however, our diagnosis shows that colonial empire has reached the point of no return and that in defending Western colonial possessions we are at best merely fighting rear-guard actions, then the United States would gain by getting ahead of events, wherever this is still possible, by speeding the process of liquidation instead of trying to hold it back like a latter-day Canute and by enlisting on its side the leaders of independence movements who, in the postwar years, for lack of sympathetic response in the West, often turned to Moscow. Such a policy would undoubtedly cause resentment in the Western colonial nations, but by no means among all groups of their population — only among those who for one personal reason or another have a stake in the retention of colonial territories.

The risk we would thus run, however, is not excessive. For it is obvious that the Western European nations must turn to the United States for military and economic aid not only for themselves but, under the Point Four program and the technical assistance projects of the United Nations, for their colonial territories as well. This does not mean that Washington should cynically use its vast financial power to coerce the colony-possessing nations into following any particular course it regards as necessary to its interests. It does mean, however, that the United States should feel free to point out, if it wishes, that certain actions on the part of Britain and France in colonial areas are not beneficial to the common interests of the North Atlantic coalition and, if necessary, should declare that it will not continue to give them assistance in the colonies to implement actions of which it disapproves. Both in Indo-China and, until recently, in Iran the United States, although in a strong position to urge reforms which many Americans — businessmen, technical experts, and missionaries — regarded as essential, hesitated to apply pressure to France and Britain until events had reached a pass where Washington had become so closely linked to the unpopular policies of the Western European nations that it had lost the possibility of exerting independent influence on native leaders.

Some Americans, on their first contact with Asia, get the impression that at least the articulate Asians are hostile to the United States and must therefore be automatically classified as pro-Russian and pro-Communist. The truth is that the peoples of Asia who have achieved independence since World War II or who are still struggling to attain it view both the United States and the U.S.S.R. primarily, and in some instances exclusively, in the context of their past and deeply resented experience with the rule of the Western colonial powers. Wherever there is hostility to the United States it stems from the impression, which it is for us to confirm or dispel, that this country, consciously or unconsciously, is helping to prolong colonial rule where it still lingers on, as in the case of French Indo-China. This hostility is particularly obvious when one sees the profound change in the attitude of the Asians toward the British now that Britain has voluntarily withdrawn from most of the areas of Asia where it had formerly held sway. Since 1945 Britain has surrendered India and Pakistan, Ceylon and Burma.

It is true that it still possesses the richest Asian colonial prize of today, Malaya, with its strategically important resources of tin and rubber — but under the impact of the postwar guerrilla warfare led by Communists, the British are now striving to give a measure of independence to the tripartite population of Malays, Chinese, and Indians, and the reform program introduced by Sir Gerald Templer and High Commissioner Malcolm MacDonald is beginning to bear fruit. As a result of this revolutionary change in the relationship of Britain to Asia, the hostility once prevalent there toward the British has for the most part disappeared, and in the area of greatest tension — India — sentiment has changed so profoundly that there is what amounts to a honeymoon between the Indians and the British.

Out of the Asians' colonial past also stems their attitude toward Russia and communism. It is important to see that attitude in the context of colonialism, and not jump to the conclusion that all Asians today are potential Communists and potential stooges of Moscow. Why has the colonial attitude affected the Asians' relations to Russia and communism? Most Americans feel that Russia is the principal enemy of the world today, and it is difficult for us to understand why the Asians are not more agitated about Russian imperialism. Why, we ask, do not Asians want openly to take their stand at our side against Russia? Are they not afraid of Russian communism? Do not Pakistan and India fear Russian invasion? Does not militant China loom darkly on the Asian horizon?

One answer to these questions is that for the Asian peoples Russia does not represent so novel a phenomenon as it does for us. They have had to deal with Russia for many years — in fact, for two centuries or more — while we have only now waked up to the fact that Russia is an Asian power. But Russia has been a great power in Asia since the eighteenth century, and the Asians do not feel that they are going to dislodge Russia from its position on the Asian continent. Their point of view is that they have to get used to living with Russia as best they can, provided Russia does not attack them. One of our most important miscalculations about foreign policy since 1945 has been due to the theory that somehow President Roosevelt "made" Russia an Asian power at Yalta. Sumner Welles, former Undersecretary of State, demolished this theory in his book *Seven Decisions That Shaped History*, where he pointed out that Russia has been a great power in Asia for at least two centuries, and that it is not within our power to make it or unmake it, but only to deal with conditions as they are.

The Indians and Pakistanis realize that Russia has been in Asia for a long time, and they became used to facing Russia throughout the nineteenth century when they were still under British rule. Russia was then regarded by Britain as a great threat to the Khyber Pass and the North-West Frontier. "The bear that walks like a man," in Rudyard Kipling's famous phrase, is not a new idea in India. What is more important for our own policy is that, as the Asians see it, Russia has never been a colonial power in Asia in a sense comparable to the position of the Western colonial powers. Therefore, when their memories react to the hated word "colonial," they react to mental pictures of Britain, the Netherlands, and France, not of Russia. True, the Russians hold vast territories in Asia, both in Central Asia and in the Far East. But these territories, long an integral part of Russia, were conquered in the eighteenth and nineteenth centuries long before Lenin and the Bolshevik party came to power. Unless we plan to fight a war to dislodge Russia from its Asian possessions, it will continue to exist as an Asian power which geographically "belongs" in Asia, as contrasted with the United States and the Western European nations, which will always be regarded as "outsiders" — good or bad outsiders, depending on their actions, but never a geographic part of the Asian continent.

Russia also has the advantage of including Asian peoples

among its citizens. Because of long experience with their own Asian population, the Russians are much closer to understanding what the Asians think than we who, seldom bothering to find out the views of the Asian peoples, usually attribute to them our own outlook. The Russians lose no time in learning the languages of Asia and establishing contacts with the peoples of Asia at what might be called the "rice-roots" level. By contrast, most of us do not speak Asian languages and therefore necessarily limit our contacts in Asia to the 10 per cent or less who speak English or French. Our knowledge of Asia is thus far more restricted than Russia's. For this we have ourselves, not the Kremlin, to blame.

It is true that at the turn of this century Russia did acquire special rights and privileges on the Asian mainland outside its own borders, notably in Manchuria. But we must always bear in mind that Russia itself was defeated by an Asian power — by Japan in the Russo-Japanese War of 1904–1905, in which, it should be recalled, the United States under Theodore Roosevelt took the side of Japan against Russia. It is important to see that war in the context of current Asian experience. For this was the first time in modern history that a white nation was defeated by an Asian power, and by siding with Japan we speeded the demise of white influence in Asia.

In the retrospect of history, it is clear that the Russo-Japanese War was the beginning of the liquidation of rule by the white man. Such position as Russia has regained in Asia since 1945, partly through the Yalta accord and partly through subsequent developments in its relations with communist China, it holds only as long as it does not try directly to coerce other nations of Asia. When it does try to do that, it will suffer the same fate as was suffered by the Western colonial powers. We can easily weaken Russia's hold on Asia as a national state by dealing fairly with the Asian peoples, by not trying to maintain the remnants of colonial rule, and by making a distinction between the

Asians' attitude toward communism and their attitude toward the Russian nation.

Many of us have become accustomed to thinking of Russia as synonymous with communism and believe that communism cannot exist unless it is attached to Russia. That is not the point of view of the thoughtful Asians. In Pakistan, for example, the Moslem religion is believed to be a great obstacle to the spread of communist ideas. Yet even in Pakistan there are political leaders who feel that they should have the right to study communism, to understand the ideas and practices of the Communists. In fact, they find in the Koran precepts which would make it possible for them to adopt certain communist practices without accepting Marxism. Why do they do all this? Because they feel that, having achieved political independence, they now should have the independence to choose the kind of economy that will be best adapted to their own needs.

There are few doctrinaire Communists in Asia as compared with Europe, where at least two generations of political leaders have been steeped in Marxist thought. In Asia one finds few convinced Marxists except in the leadership of China. What one finds is a profound interest as to how the ideas and practices of communism might speed the economic development of backward areas.

In addressing ourselves to the Asians we often give the impression that the Indians or the Chinese are Americans who somehow went wrong and who should be brought back into the fold by our propaganda. All too often the only reaction we get to our descriptions of American wealth is the not unnatural attitude of Asians who say: "Well, if the United States is so rich, you can give your stuff away — and you don't even deserve gratitude, for you are merely handing over what you do not need."

Yet Asia does not want charity from us, or gifts out of our surplus riches, but solid and substantial aid for the development of a viable economy which is essential to future political stability. The underdeveloped nations need American financial and technical aid and, contrary to the impression prevailing in some quarters, are eager to obtain it — but they want to obtain it on their own terms.

This does not mean that they object to reasonable safeguards about supervision of the way in which aid is utilized and distributed. What they resent is any indication that the American government or American business interests will offer aid on conditions that would be regarded as an infringement on the right of new nations to shape their political, economic, and social institutions as they see fit. Here, again, colonial experience casts a long shadow on relations with the United States. If the suggestion is made, no matter how diplomatically, that more generous aid would be forthcoming, either in the form of American governmental loans or larger private investments if underdeveloped country X would reject socialism and introduce free private enterprise, or if it granted special safeguards to Americans, then negotiations are threatened with failure. If, however, Americans, both officials and private citizens, recognize, that other nations, with a history of economic development vastly different from our own, may want to follow patterns unfamiliar and even unacceptable to us, then a wide margin for agreement can be found in the underdeveloped areas.

The leaders of former or existing colonial territories understand that the American government and American private investors will want to have some assurance that gifts, loans, credits, or investments are put to good use, without discrimination, and not appropriated by a few members of the ruling group or dissipated on unconstructive projects, as happened with American aid to Chiang Kai-shek. In their present state of sensitivity concerning relations between the great powers and the colonies, however, they often find it difficult to accept

supervision by the United States alone, whether officials dis-
bursing government aid or private concerns seeking sound investments for their capital.

United States aid to the underdeveloped areas of Asia and
the Middle East takes and can continue to take various forms.
It can be given out of government resources provided by the
taxpayers, as under the Point Four program inaugurated in 1949
and allocations under the Mutual Security Program adopted in
1951. It can be offered in the form of a cooperative effort between the government and private investors, as Washington
intends to do under Point Four and certain operations of the
Mutual Security Program. It can be provided through American governmental grants to programs formulated by other
Western nations in cooperation with some of the countries of
Asia, notably under the Colombo plan. It can be furnished
directly to governments which, for one reason or another, have
peculiarly close relations with the United States, notably the
Philippines. Or it can be channeled through the agencies of the
United Nations concerned with technical assistance to under-
developed areas.

The Point Four program announced in President Truman's
inaugural address of January 20, 1949, became law on June 5,
1950, as "An Act for International Development." This act
empowered the President to proceed with the technical-
assistance phase of the plan for raising the level of industrialization in the underdeveloped areas through governmental aid.
The Administration also proposed under the Point Four program to encourage the flow of private capital abroad by tax
concessions and guarantees against losses on foreign investments
arising from expropriation or currency inconvertibility.

Three appropriations were made by Congress to cover the
cost of the Point Four program for the fiscal years ending June
30, 1951, 1952, and 1953. The three appropriations, excluding
funds for special relief programs in Israel, amounted in the

respective years to $35.4 million, $147.9 million, and $155.6 million, making a total of $338 million. These amounts include the annual $12-million contribution of the United States to the $26-million technical assistance program of the United Nations, as well as its contribution to the long-established activities of the Institute of Inter-American Affairs which have been frequently described as a "preview of Point Four." Excluding these items, the funds which were made available for Point Four operations in the underdeveloped countries in the three years were $16.8 million, $126.9 million, and $138.9 million, respectively.

The Department of State is responsible by executive order for the operation of Point Four. Coordination with other foreign economic programs is provided by the director of the Mutual Security Agency (MSA), successor to the Economic Cooperation Administration (ECA) whose activities were terminated on December 31, 1951. Two basic techniques are used in providing technical assistance to underdeveloped countries. Qualified American specialists, with necessary demonstration or teaching equipment, are sent to the host countries to help the people in their own communities; and professional people, technicians, and skilled workers from the countries receiving aid are brought for training here. Training is given in agricultural, technical, and professional schools, in private industry and research institutions, and in specialized fields in government agencies. The trainees, after learning American organization, methods, and skills, return to their countries for practical application of their training. As of September 1, 1952, there were 614 Point Four trainees from 35 countries in the United States, the largest number of whom were receiving training in agriculture.

At the present time Point Four projects are in operation in 35 of the 38 independent countries in the Middle East, Asia, and Latin America. As of September 1, 1952, there were 1,500

Americans in 35 countries working on Point Four projects, with more technicians working in agriculture than in any other field.

From the outset, the Point Four program has labored under the handicap of being originally presented in such glowing terms as a "bold new program" that it was easy for the American public as well as for recipients of aid to overlook the fact that it was essentially a long-term policy of guided self-help. In the underdeveloped areas, Point Four was often considered as a sort of super give-away, and invidious comparisons were drawn between the relatively modest sums allocated for the nonindustrialized nations and the vast sums spent by the United States under the Marshall Plan for the economies of the already industrialized nations of Western Europe. When the meaning of the Point Four program was eventually understood by the underdeveloped countries, their initial reaction was one of profound disappointment. Prime Minister Jawaharlal Nehru of India at that time said the program was of "no great value," and M. A. H. Ispahani, Pakistan ambassador to the United States, termed it financially inadequate.

The United States, undismayed, proceeded to negotiate a number of variously devised bilateral agreements designed to implement Point Four. These negotiations have led to a clearer understanding of the program as well as to a more friendly attitude on the part of the prospective recipients. The first comprehensive and integrated project under the Point Four program was concluded by the United States with Iran in October 1950 and involved an allocation of $500,000 to help improve conditions in rural Iran. Under the project villagers were to be taught elementary sanitation and agricultural and vocational techniques in centrally located demonstration centers. It was hoped that this mass education would, among other things, reduce the number, about 4 million, who fall victim to malaria every year.

Unlike the Iranian agreement, the "umbrella" Point Four arrangement with Ceylon does not involve a grant of funds. Instead it prescribes methods of technical cooperation, including certain projects, and specifies the conditions that must be met to qualify the island for Point Four funds. Liberia has received an allocation of $850,000 to finance the activities of American technicians working in the fields of health, agriculture, power, transport, and public administration. The Point Four agreement concluded with Brazil on October 23, 1952, provides for joint work in developing Brazil's medium and light industries. In this case the United States, through the Institute of Inter-American Affairs, will furnish technical personnel and $160,000 of the first year's operating costs. Brazil, for its part, agreed to invest $400,000.

In each case — and each agreement is adapted as much as possible to the particular needs of the recipient country — the government receiving aid undertakes to provide approximately the dollar equivalent of the Point Four funds in goods and services to be utilized in connection with local projects. It is estimated, for example, that Iran's contribution of experts, equipment, buildings, and land would involve a local outlay valued at $4 for every dollar provided by the United States.

It will thus be seen that the Point Four program, which is intended to meet the needs of 35 countries in three major areas of the world, does not represent a major financial commitment comparable to the Marshall Plan for Europe. The modest dimension of the Point Four expenditure, in fact, has been one of the principal targets of criticism by the underdeveloped nations. Other criticisms are that the program of technical assistance does not provide for capital aid required for the adequate financing of projects recommended by Point Four experts (it was partly on this ground that Syria, in October 1952, declined to accept a $10-million Point Four grant from the United States); that many American technicians are inadequately prepared to deal with conditions in nonindustrialized areas and expect to enjoy living standards so much in excess of the average as to excite resentment on the part of the local populations; and that American ideas as to the objectives of reorganizing and modernizing underdeveloped economies are often sharply at variance with the objectives of local political and economic leaders.

It is true that many Americans, unaccustomed to the problems of nonindustrialized economies, made serious mistakes in the early stages of the Point Four program. However, some, at least, have learned through harsh experience that, if they are to succeed and, through their success, enhance the prestige of the United States abroad, they will have to approach their tasks not as zealous reformers who attempt to remake other nations in the image of America but as men and women sensitive to local needs and dedicated to the idea that their job is to help other peoples fulfill their aspirations on their own terms.

Another criticism made by recipients of United States aid is that Americans are more interested in obtaining the strategic materials of underdeveloped countries than in advancing the welfare of their peoples. President Truman sought to dispel this criticism when, in his message to Congress in September 1951, he said: "The conditions of the people in the underdeveloped areas would be a matter of humanitarian concern even if our national security were not involved. Major improvement in these conditions is necessarily a long-term process in which their countries' own efforts, private investments, and public developmental loans should play the largest part. Carefully selected projects of technical assistance and initial development on a grant basis, however, can speed up this process and provide tangible benefits even in the short run." But no matter how good the intentions of the United States, the fact must be faced that the understandable desire of this country and of the other industrial nations of the West to obtain raw materials for their factories, in time of peace as well as in time of cold war, may not always harmonize with the also understandable desire of the nonindustrialized peoples to retain a larger share of their raw materials than in the past for the modernization and development of their own economies. The United States and the underdeveloped peoples agree about the need for development. They may not always see eye to eye about the principal goals such development should achieve. A great deal of patience and mutual understanding will be required if controversy on this score is to be avoided.

In addition to the Point Four program, the United States, under the Mutual Security Program of 1951, made allocations — primarily to strengthen arms preparedness — to underdeveloped areas as follows: for Asia, $375 million in economic and $555 million in military aid (Asia meaning the Far East); for the Middle East and North Africa $125 million in economic and $415 million in military aid; for Latin America $22 million in economic and $40 million in military aid. The bulk of military aid in the Middle East was to go to Greece and Turkey — in continuation of the Truman Doctrine program initiated in 1947 — and to Iran. The military aid voted for the Far East was to be divided among the Chinese Nationalists on Formosa, the French anti-communist native forces in Indo-China, and the armies of the Philippines and Thailand. In announcing economic aid for the Middle East, the Administration took the occasion to advocate the development of good relations between Israel and the Arab states, saying: "The fundamental requirement is a regional approach to the basic problems of economic development . . . urgently needed to reduce existing tensions, especially through the orderly settlement of homeless (Arab) refugees." However, aside from continuation of the existing refugee program, recognized as inadequate, the drafters of the program set forth no plan to make possible the "regional approach." The linking of military to economic aid under the

Mutual Security Program created delicate problems in aid negotiations with some underdeveloped countries, notably Indonesia, which would welcome American economic assistance but
regard acceptance of military assistance as an undesirable political commitment that might oblige them to take sides openly
in the cold war between the West and the U.S.S.R.

Another source of financial aid to underdeveloped areas from
American governmental sources has been the Export-Import
Bank. During 1951, 96 per cent of the $395 million lent by the
Bank went to underdeveloped countries, with the law requiring
that loans be granted for projects that could not be financed
through normal commercial channels. The Bank's 1951 loans
included power projects in Cuba; roads, water supply, and
sewage systems in Liberia; Diesel locomotives in Uruguay and
Colombia; airports in Ecuador; and a dam in Haiti.

American industrialists and bankers have complained that the
United States, under the Point Four, MSA, and Export-Import
Bank programs, has placed too much emphasis on government
loans and grants and has neglected the possibilities of assisting
private American investments in underdeveloped areas. In recent years the American economy has offered such a lucrative
field for investment that the opportunities for American capital
in other areas of the world, most of which have been in a state
of ferment, have offered little temptation. Now as defense expenditures taper off here, many proposals are being made for
initiating investments in areas where they are nonexistent and
expanding them where they are already under way. Energetic
programs for pushing economic development in Latin America
particularly, but also in some sectors of the Middle East and
Asia, have been presented by various private groups. In October
1952 the National Planning Association announced that it was
undertaking a study for the purpose of developing a pattern
that would enable United States industry to play a decisive
part in aiding the economic progress of the less developed coun-

tries, with consequent benefits to the entire free world. Well-informed American industrialists and bankers now recognize that in the past they had not always shown adequate attention to native interests, and are ready to improve their policies in the future, provided the countries in which they invest guarantee the safety of their investments and provided that the United States government forgoes double taxation.

While welcoming aid directly given by the United States, either through government or private channels, the Asian nations have also shown lively interest in obtaining financial and technical assistance from Britain and other members of the British Commonwealth of Nations. On November 29, 1950, seven Commonwealth countries — Australia, Canada, Ceylon, India, New Zealand, Pakistan, and Britain — announced the six-year Colombo plan for economic development of South and Southeast Asia. This plan provides for the establishment of an organization composed both of countries supplying capital and countries receiving it, which would review progress, draw up periodic reports, and serve as a forum for the discussion of development problems in the region. Agriculture, transport and communications, and electric power, regarded as the basic development requirements, account for over 70 per cent of the total expenditure of $5 billion contemplated in the Colombo plan, with 10 per cent allocated to industry and 10 per cent to "social capital" — housing, health, and education.

The Colombo nations fully realize that their plan will require for its fulfillment substantial aid by the United States, and it is their hope that this country will participate in the proposed organization. The advantage of the Colombo plan, from the point of view of the Asian nations, is that it provides machinery to assure joint, instead of bilateral, negotiations by the industrial and underdeveloped countries, for the simultaneous economic and social development of areas of Asia on a basis of equality between former colonial powers and former

colonies. So great is the attraction of this scheme of joint development that non-Commonwealth nations of Southeast Asia
— Burma, Indonesia, and Vietnam — have indicated their intention to participate in the Colombo plan.

Still another approach, again bilateral, to the economic problems of underdeveloped countries is found in the report of the
Economic Survey Mission to the Philippines in 1950, com-
monly known as the Bell report * because the mission, composed of industrialists, bankers, economists, and representatives
of labor, was headed by Daniel Bell, a banker and former
Undersecretary of the Treasury. This report bluntly pointed
out that "the basic economic problem in the Philippines is in-
efficient production and very low economy." It chided the
Philippine government, which had gained independence in
1946 as promised by the United States, for its failure to expand
production and to increase productive efficiency, in spite of the
fact that investment was exceptionally large during most of the
post-liberation period.

While the Bell report did not directly make this point, its
criticism of the Philippine government was, in effect, a criticism
of colonial economy in general — and thus, in retrospect, a
criticism also of the manner in which the United States, during
the period of American administration, 1899–1946, had on the
whole perpetuated the colonial structure of the Philippine economy. The material destruction wrought by war and Japanese
conquest must, of course, be taken into consideration in apprais-
ing the economic situation in the Philippine Islands. The suc-
cinct analysis of the Bell mission, however, is relevant to the
problems of other colonial areas, including those which have
not experienced the ravages of war.

"Too much of the investment," was the report, "went into
commerce and real estate instead of the development of agri-

* *Report to the President of the United States by the Economic Survey Mission to the Philippines* (Washington, D.C., October 9, 1950).

culture and industry; investment undertaken by Government corporations has unfortunately been ineffective. A considerable part of the large foreign exchange receipts were dissipated in imports of luxury and nonessential goods, in the remittance of high profits, and in the transfer of Philippine capital abroad. The opportunity to increase productive efficiency and to raise the standard of living in the Philippines in the postwar period has thus been wasted because of misdirected investment and excessive imports for consumption.

"The inequalities in income in the Philippines, always large, have become even greater during the past few years. While the standard of living of the mass of people has not reached the prewar level, the profits of businessmen and the incomes of large landowners have risen very considerably. Wages and farm income remain lower than the economy can afford because of the unequal bargaining power of workers and tenants on the one hand, and employers and landowners on the other. Under such conditions any policy that keeps prices high has the effect of transferring real income from the poor to the rich. . . .

"The high hopes of the Philippine people that with peace and independence, they could look forward to economic progress and a rising standard of living have not been realized. Because of the deteriorating economic situation, there is a widespread feeling of disillusion. Most agricultural and industrial workers have no faith that their economic position can or will be improved. Businessmen fear a collapse of the peace. The uncertainties created by these doubts are strengthened by the recent tendency toward unemployment resulting from the slowing up of construction and the sharp curtailment of imports. The economy shows little inherent capacity to overcome the difficulties with which it is faced. . . .

"Inefficiency and even corruption in the Government service are widespread. Leaders in agriculture and in business have not been sufficiently aware of their responsibility to improve the economic position of the lower income groups. The public lacks confidence in the capacity of the Government to act firmly to protect the interests of all the people."

This situation, the Bell mission recognized, "is being exploited by the Communist-led Hukbalahap movement to incite lawlessness and disorder." What remedy should be provided under the circumstances? Instead of concentrating on efforts to fight the Huks by force, which until then had been the program of the Philippine government, the Bell mission attacked the causes of the disease, not merely its symptoms. "A permanent solution to these problems," it declared, "will be found only through a determined effort on the part of the people and the Government of the Philippines, with the aid and encouragement of the United States, to increase production and improve productive efficiency, to raise the level of wages and farm income, and to open new opportunities for work and for acquiring land."

To achieve these objectives, the Bell mission recommended measures that, if urged by governments or political parties in other countries, might be regarded by many Americans as revolutionary in character. The mission proposed revision of the tax structure to increase the proportion of taxes collected from high incomes and large property holdings; redistribution of land through the purchase of large estates for resale to small farmers; diversification of the Islands' economy by encouraging new industries; the establishment of a Philippine Development Corporation to coordinate all government enterprises; reexamination of practices with respect to the use of the public domain; a special two-year emergency tax of 25 per cent on imports other than those of essential foods and of fertilizer in order to reduce "the excessive demand" for imports; establishment through appropriate legislation of the right of workers to organize free trade unions to protect their economic interests; an adequate program of public health and improved education, and better facilities for urban housing; provision for more efficient distribution facilities so as to lower prices to consumers and increase returns to producers; and improvement and reorganization of public administration so as to ensure honesty and efficiency in government.

Two features of the Bell report are of particular significance for the future relations of the United States with underdeveloped areas. First, in the opinion of the mission, "it is clear that the Government will have to take an active part in stimulating economic development in the Philippines. It will have to provide much of the planning and some of the construction for major enterprises. It will have to help private enterprise with technical assistance. It will have to give financial assistance to stimulate private investment in the industrial fields of special importance to the economy. Precisely because of the large part that will have to be undertaken by the Government, it is important that its functions in this field be clear, and that it be prepared to perform these functions with honesty and efficiency." This acknowledgment of the role that government initiative must play, now and in the immediate future, in the planned development of the resources and skills of underdeveloped areas, represents a new element in the thinking of Americans concerned with foreign-policy problems, who in the past had given the impression that they expected colonial or semi-colonial areas to introduce the practice of free enterprise overnight and had frowned on all talk of planning. Should the Bell mission's acknowledgment of the role of government in underdeveloped economies become an official feature of American policy, one of the most serious obstacles to understanding between the United States and the leaders of Asian and Middle Eastern nations would be promptly removed.

Second, the Bell mission recommended that American funds amounting to $250 million to help the Philippines carry out a five-year program of economic development and technical assistance be granted only after the fundamental reforms it suggested had been effected by the Philippine government. It insisted, also, that "expenditure from United States loans and grants be subject to continued supervision of the Technical Mission" to be appointed by Washington, thereby introducing the feature of strict supervision which had hitherto been lacking in American financial aid to countries of Asia and the Middle East.

While this recommendation of the Bell mission was severely criticized by Manila newspapers reflecting the view of President Elpidio Quirino as an unacceptable encroachment on national sovereignty, it was finally accepted after American spokesmen had pointed out that the Western countries receiving Marshall Plan aid had complied with comparable conditions under the Economic Cooperation Administration. The supervision conditions, however, provoked little opposition outside government circles, and thoughtful Filipinos were prompt to say that they thought a system of strict accounting offered the only safeguard against the possibility that a corrupt administration might dissipate American funds without in any way benefiting the population. It is heartening for us to know that the only Asian nation which has had direct experience with American rule preferred to accept United States, rather than United Nations, supervision.

This, however, is by no means universally true of the nations of Asia and the Middle East which are still smarting under the recollection of Western colonial rule. Their leaders, when they speak frankly, declare that they would prefer to have United States aid, under the Point Four and other programs, channeled through the United Nations and the specialized agencies. Such a procedure, they believe, would have two advantages. First, this would make it possible for the recipients of aid to draw on the services of experts from various countries

— not only from the United States, as must be done under the Point Four and other bilateral programs — some of whom, because of past experience in conditions comparable to those of underdeveloped areas, might prove more immediately helpful, and also less costly, than American experts who have acquired their knowledge and skills in an environment which cannot be easily duplicated elsewhere. At the same time, this would make the recipients of aid feel that they have a certain leeway in framing their own development programs. Second, supervision by United Nations commissions, composed of citizens of other UN members as well as the United States, would give the American taxpayers assurance that the aid they supply has been effectively used. Thus the natural sensitivities of both giver and recipient could be adequately satisfied.

The desirability of international supervision was stressed in 1951 by a group of experts appointed by Trygve Lie, Secretary-General of the United Nations, to examine measures for the economic development of underdeveloped countries. This group, composed of representatives from the United States, Britain, India, Chile, and Lebanon, stated in its report * that $19 billion a year for five years would be needed to achieve an annual net increase of 2 per cent in the national income of underdeveloped countries, 80 per cent of which would be needed by the countries of Southeast Asia and the Far East. This figure has been seriously questioned by some experts in the United States, who consider it altogether too high and who contend that even if the funds were available, which they doubt, many of the underdeveloped countries are not in a position to absorb and make use of such large financial resources.

The UN experts acknowledge that the amount they specify

---

* *Measures for the Economic Development of Underdeveloped Countries*, Report by a Group of Experts appointed by the Secretary-General of the United Nations. (United Nations, Department of Economic Affairs, New York, May 1951.)

is large in relation to the past history of underdeveloped areas, where the annual inflow of external capital in the 1920s averaged not more than $500 million a year and where the current inflow is approximately $1,500 million, including all loans and grants. They point out, however, that a highly developed country like the United States has a net annual investment of $25 to $30 billion a year "for a population one-tenth the size of that which we are considering, and for an economy that is already highly developed." (The paucity of funds available for the development of underdeveloped areas as compared with funds granted the advanced industrial nations of Western Europe under the Marshall Plan and other aid programs is regarded in Asia as a sign of economic discrimination against non-European countries.) The UN experts contend, moreover, that if the United States, Canada, Australasia, and the countries of Western Europe, with an aggregate national income of about $350 billion a year, were to transfer 2 per cent of this amount annually to the underdeveloped countries, this would be equal to $7 billion a year. "Neither would this be a very high target," the report continues. "In 1905–1913, the United Kingdom exported capital to the extent of an annual average of £143 million, which was 7 per cent of her annual national income. And, similarly, loans and grants from the United States of America have been running at over 3 per cent of her national income in the past five years."

The UN experts recommend the establishment by the United Nations of an International Development Authority with power to make grants to governments of underdeveloped countries for nonproductive purposes for which commercial resources are usually not available — notably agricultural expansion services, education and research, public-health programs emphasizing preventive medicine and nutrition rather than curative medicine, subsidization of medium- and short-term farm credit, and improvement of rural public works, such as roads, rural water supplies, land reclamation, drainage, soil conservation, and afforestation.

The issue of international supervision over the expenditure of international grants is squarely faced by the UN experts. In commenting on the advantage of an international body over a national body for the development of nonindustrialized economies, they declare that "international verification of expenditures is more acceptable to the receiving countries." Even so, "a political issue of some delicacy arises with international verification," for "some countries are ruled by corrupt or reactionary cliques whose regime might be overthrown by the people if there were no foreign aid, and who may be settled in their rule because foreign grants have become available." The UN experts express the hope that "the United Nations will not wish to have had any hand in fastening such governments on peoples. They might therefore wish to lay down certain minimum conditions before an underdeveloped country was admitted to the list of those eligible to receive grants."

At present the underdeveloped countries are receiving a modest but effective amount of direct aid from the United Nations under a technical assistance program administered by the Economic and Social Council and implemented by various international agencies, notably the Food and Agriculture Organization. The members of the United Nations contribute funds to this technical assistance program — the share of the United States, as already noted, being $12.5 million a year out of an estimated $26-million budget. As of September 1, 1952, the United Nations had 1,400 technical experts in 53 countries and had provided training for more than 1,600 fellows from 69 countries.

Some American observers believe that the United States would benefit by channeling as much of its appropriations for technical assistance as possible through the UN agencies. The argument often made here that such aid would be subject to the veto of the U.S.S.R. — the same argument was invoked to keep the Marshall Plan project out of the United Nations in 1947 — is groundless. In the eighteen-nation Economic and Social Council of the UN, which deals with technical assistance, no member has the veto; nor is there a right of veto in the UN General Assembly, where decisions are taken by a two-thirds majority. Moreover, technical assistance to underdeveloped areas is the one issue on which there has been overwhelming agreement in the UN, and Russia raised no objections to the Point Four program when Washington, in urging technical assistance, discussed it in the Economic and Social Council in 1949.

Within the UN system the United States has authorized the International Bank for Reconstruction and Development to lend its full paid-in American subscription of $635 million and to raise further dollar funds by bond issues in this country. As of 1952, the Bank, with $1,500,000,000 in 72 loans, was helping to finance 250 projects in 28 countries. The Bank has concentrated on such basic projects as agricultural production in the Belgian Congo; electric power in Brazil, Colombia, Iceland, Yugoslavia, and Uruguay; roads, ports, and railways in Australia, Ethiopia, Nicaragua, and Turkey; flood control and irrigation in Iraq and Thailand; and grain storage in Nicaragua and Turkey. The Bank has frequently been criticized for what is regarded as its exaggerated cautiousness in making loans to underdeveloped countries unless it can be convinced that such loans represent a sound banking risk — when, it is argued, many projects for new development in nonindustrialized countries must by definition be fraught with all kinds of risks. At its Mexico City conference of September 1952, the Bank indicated that henceforth it would take a broader view of risk-entailing commitments than in the past; and at the *New York Herald Tribune* Forum in October of that year, Eugene Black, president of the Bank, declared that the world's industrialized countries will need to supply steady financial aid to the underdeveloped nations for many years to come. He also called for outright grants to some poorer countries and the removal of all unnecessary trade restrictions.

If out of the various types of aid — bilateral, regional, and international — which are now being considered or have actually been put into operation, we can evolve some formula for rapidly developing the Asian economies by democratic methods, without resort to dictatorship and forced labor, then we shall have met our principal challenge in Asia. But in looking for that formula, we must never forget that the Asians have not been brought up in a Western tradition: they do not have our background of political liberty; they have lived for centuries under the authoritarian rule of colonial powers who were real despots, no matter how benevolent and enlightened their despotism; and they must not be expected to achieve Western technology in short order.

The economic and social problems of nations most of whom have only recently emerged from colonial rule and are struggling to bridge the gap that separates them from the West are greatly complicated by continued political uncertainty, particularly in the Far East. There, Russia, China, and Japan — rivals for power since the end of the nineteenth century — are once more girding for a showdown, with Korea, long a bone of contention between them, again at stake, and the United States, backed by the United Nations, playing a major part in the struggle. In Asia, as in Europe, the United States has inherited the role once played by Britain and is becoming the keystone of a Pacific coalition in which it would safeguard Australia, New Zealand, and the Philippines against Russia and China, but also, in another eventuality, against a remilitarized Japan. In this coalition Britain, to its dismay, has hitherto not been invited to play a significant part.

It is difficult to see how the struggle for power in the Far

East, whose military aspects have so far been limited to the Korean War and the guerrilla fighting in Indo-China and Malaya, can be resolved unless a series of decisions going far beyond a Korean truce is reached. The Korean War, devastating as its human losses are for both sides, gives both sides strategic advantages. The West believes that as long as large Chinese forces are pinned down in Korea they cannot move elsewhere in Asia. The Communists, for their part, apparently find it convenient to hold in Korea large American forces which might otherwise be available for service in Europe, the Middle East, or some other sensitive area.

If a truce is at all feasible, it could be achieved only through over-all negotiations about all outstanding Far Eastern problems. Russia and China, which for over fifty years have regarded Korea as a bridgehead for Japanese invasion of their territories, would not surrender Korea to the West, as represented by the United States or the United Nations, unless Japan could in some way be rendered innocuous and Chiang Kai-shek, who continues to hope for return to the China mainland, would withdraw from Formosa. For its part, the United States in the past fifty years has regarded Russia and Japan alternatively as a threat to American security, and would not abandon its present preferential position in Japan, its safeguards of Formosa, and its defense of Korea unless it could be assured that Russia and China no longer represent a menace to Asia and to this country.

This gigantic deadlock may not be broken in the near future, but it may be gradually chipped away by a variety of moves, over some of which we shall have little control. Japan, whose economy, deficient in raw materials and peculiarly dependent on export trade, has been sustained largely through American aid since the war, would find itself in a perilous position with the end of the Korean campaign. The Japanese are already contesting markets claimed by Britain, which also needs desperately to export, in southeast Asia and in western Africa. Sooner or later they will either clash with the British or will have to trade with China, whose Manchurian raw-material resources had formerly helped to feed Japanese industries. Once Japan starts doing business with China, it will be difficult for the United States to ignore the Peiping regime. It is impossible for Washington to recognize Peiping, or accept its admission to the United Nations, as long as the Korean War continues. A truce, however, would reopen the Pandora box of troubles by raising anew the questions of the status of Formosa, the future of Chiang Kai-shek, and American relations with Mao Tse-tung. Whatever one's political convictions, it is difficult to believe that the Peiping regime can be overthrown by an invasion from outside organized around Chiang Kai-shek, any more than it proved possible in the past thirty years to overthrow the Soviet government in Russia by outside pressures. The United States may legitimately insist on safeguards about the use of Formosa and other adjacent strategic islands by the Chinese Communists, but it would probably be in a better position if it placed these safeguards, as it has the military operations in Korea, under the auspices of the United Nations, instead of maintaining them on a unilateral basis. Meanwhile, the United States could avoid possible fissures in the Western coalition by encouraging Britain, in spite of its reduced military strength, to participate to the fullest degree possible in the activities of a Pacific union. And it could avert criticism of its policies in Asia by publicly urging the French to proceed more rapidly than in the past with their announced plans to give the Vietnam government independence, and to make clear their intention of withdrawing from Indo-China once the guerrilla war is over.

As important as an understanding of the economic and political problems faced by underdeveloped areas in their belated industrial revolution, is an understanding of the misgivings created in the minds of the world's non-white majority by what they know of the racist attitude of Americans. Nothing can work so much against the United States in Asia — not to speak of Africa — as any indication of discrimination on the ground of color. We must get used to the idea that the majority of the peoples of the world, and the majority of the nations of the United Nations, are going to be, over the long run, non-white nations. The sooner we get used to this idea, the better it will be for us and for our children. When Japan proclaimed the slogan of "Asia for the Asians," it was appealing to a deep-seated emotion in Asia. Had the Japanese been less ruthless in their treatment of the peoples they conquered, they might well have succeeded in their attack on the white man. As it is, the Japanese gravely and, in some cases, perhaps irretrievably undermined white prestige in Asia.

There is no need to dwell on the picture of racial tensions between whites and Negroes in the United States as depicted by communist, but also to some extent by non-communist, French and British propaganda: a picture compounded of slave labor, lynchings that go unpunished, discriminations at all levels of society and in all spheres of activity, and interracial resentments ready to flare up into dangerous conflicts at any moment. We can easily counter this picture by giving a factual account of the remarkable progress achieved in relations between whites and Negroes during the past quarter of a century, most of all in the South. We can point to the steady broadening of political, economic, and educational opportunities for Negroes; the constant struggle on the part of the white population against discrimination; the high sense of responsibility and steadfast loyalty of our Negro fellow citizens who have not succumbed to communist propaganda even under stress of grievous provocations. In the field of interracial relations, as in the field of economic and social developments in general, the United States has experienced a revolution the scope of which we ourselves do not always fully realize, and which we have not yet succeeded in describing adequately to other peoples.

We have a magnificent story to tell which is creditable to both whites and Negroes. Nevertheless, again and again episodes occur which mar and distort this story not only in our own eyes but, what is more important, in the eyes of the millions of non-whites in Asia, the Middle East, Africa, and Latin America which are now focused on the United States. The rear-guard struggle waged in a few states of the South against equality of educational opportunities of the Negroes — and waged not by ignorant "poor whites" but by political leaders like Governor James F. Byrnes of South Carolina, a former Secretary of State; the recurring discrimination, with Negroes severely punished for deeds on true or trumped-up charges which are readily dismissed when made against whites accused of injuring Negroes; and upsurges of racial hatred that reveal, in a grim flash, the impulses of cruelty and irrationality endemic in every society, as in the 1951 riots of Cicero, Illinois — all these, magnified by reports carried in the press of non-white nations, revive the fear that the United States, no matter how excellent its intentions, will in practice pursue a policy inimical to the interests of peoples of another color.

The social discrimination traditionally practiced by the British in the heyday of their empire, and practiced not only among the less developed tribes of darkest Africa but also toward the political and cultural leaders of India and China, was probably one of the most important factors in undermining the influence of Britain in the colonial areas. What has been called the *mem-sahib* complex of the British, their insistence on barring "natives," no matter how well-educated and politically responsible, from clubs, hotels, and other places of social contact — this has been done until recently in Malaya where Britain is engaged in a life-and-death struggle with communist guerrillas — could not but convince farsighted leaders of Asia and the

Middle East that no matter how adept they might become in the skills of Western technical civilization, they would still remain, under British rule, "second-class" citizens. They would still be regarded as fit only to serve as clerks of their white masters and be condemned to living in the ghettos assigned to them by British social custom, which, in turn, was set by the narrow-minded conventions of Britain's conservative middle class of the nineteenth century.

While Americans may appear more flexible socially — our social mobility is perhaps the aspect of our way of life which arouses the greatest admiration in Asia — we are now actually regarded as today's potential threat to the ultimate position of the non-white peoples. For the attitude of condescension, of "father knows best," which the British and other European colonial rulers had adopted toward the "barbarians" whom they regarded as "the white man's burden," has been consciously or unconsciously taken over by many Americans in colonial areas where the British have surrendered their former dominance.

Not only do Americans who go to Asia on business or official assignments expect special privileges and comforts which are not available to their opposite numbers among the natives, but in the discussion of world problems the United States still tends to pay far less attention to the views of non-white than of white nations. For example, the Department of State consistently discounted the suggestions offered by Prime Minister Nehru in 1950, during the Korean crisis and the subsequent entrance of communist China into the Korean War. It waved aside the objections of the Philippines to the Japanese peace treaty, when the Filipinos, whose friendship to this country is not questioned, contended that Japan should be made to take some responsibility for the damage it had wreaked on the islands by paying reparations. It underrated the strength of Iran's nationalist desire for independence from political intervention by

Britain. Nor have the non-white peoples of the world been reassured by the lukewarm attitude of the United States toward the fiercely racist program of the government of Prime Minister Malan in the Union of South Africa. Under this program — clearly inspired by the example of the Nazis — which creates a ghetto life for the non-whites who constitute a majority of the population, the Malan government hopes to safeguard the supremacy of the white European minority and erect a permanent barrier to the tide of independence sentiment now rising among the African populations. As Lillian Smith, author of *Strange Fruit,* has pointed out, a great nation like the United States which still hangs signs on many doors differentiating between *White* and *Colored* must be prepared to have its ultimate objectives questioned by even the most friendly colored peoples outside its borders.

There are still too few Westerners who realize that contempt, whether explicit or implied, toward the cultures of non-Western peoples represents a far greater threat to our ultimate security in a predominantly non-white world than the danger currently created by Russian imperialism or communist conspiracy. This threat was grimly pointed out by a reporter for the Canadian Press in a dispatch from Korea published in the *New York Herald Tribune* of August 19, 1951, who said:

"Indoctrination would have avoided the superiority complex into which UN troops have fallen here. The Korean people have been so humiliated by the universal contemptuous attitude, the sneering arrogance that springs from treating humans like cattle, that experienced observers fear they have irretrievably alienated them. Said one foreign correspondent with years abroad for a United States newspaper: 'It doesn't matter now who wins the war. Our troops have lost us the Koreans.' "

The most important step we can take toward making friends for America in non-white areas of the world is to abandon our attitude of tolerance toward peoples who differ from us in

color — would we like to be merely tolerated by non-whites?
— and deal with them on a basis of equality, which means equality in recognizing our respective achievements and failings. Tolerance is a form of condescension which can no longer be practiced by Westerners with impunity. Dr. Herrymon Maurer,
a Quaker, in his stimulating book, *Collision of East and West,**
rightly states that "during the past twenty-five years the conflict of East and West has been attended not so much by obvious
economic exploitation as by hidden mental condescension. This
condescension took the form of a one-way communication
of ideas, a type of communication that usually fails unless it
is backed by force." It might be added that the use of force,
as in the case of British rule in India, obviously prevents communication, instead of promoting it. Now that the British have
withdrawn, now that Britain has been shorn of the panoply
of imperial power, the Indians find many things to admire in
British ideas and practices which had previously seemed to
them not merely alien but also hostile and hateful. What we
need to do in Asia, and other underdeveloped areas which have
suffered for centuries from Western condescension, is to establish two-way communication — to indicate, in a spirit of humility, that we have something to learn as well as something to
teach.

Here again, as with the need for social progress in Western
Europe, an ounce of prevention through timely enlightened
action at home and abroad would be worth many pounds of
cure in the form of extensive propaganda. What Dr. Gunnar
Myrdal, the Swedish sociologist, has called "The American
Dilemma" of relations between whites and Negroes within
our own borders has been expanded to world dimensions now
that the United States has assumed the leadership of the non-
communist nations and has inherited the manifold problems

* Herrymon Maurer, *Collision of East and West* (Regnery, Chicago,
1951).

whose handling by the European colonial powers was once the subject of vigorous American criticism. A great moral test faces us in Asia. For if we can learn to act with a sense of responsibility, with a feeling not of mere tolerance but of understanding of the problems of non-white peoples, with the realization that on a democratic basis of equality these peoples constitute the majority of the world community and will henceforth claim an increasing share of participation in world affairs, then we will not only gradually win the confidence of Asia, the Middle East, Africa, and Latin America, but also blaze new trails for the peaceful coexistence of different racial groups on a world scale.

Our challenge in Asia is to help newly independent peoples and peoples still striving for independence to carry out the First Industrial Revolution, which took place in the West a hundred and fifty years ago, in Russia only at the end of the nineteenth century, and is now being telescoped, in Russia and Asia, with vast political and social changes. Our task is to help carry out this First Industrial Revolution by democratic methods, without the human and material hardships imposed by the communist dictatorships in Russia and China, and with due regard for racial dignity, so long unrecognized by the West, and to prove in the course of it that our methods can bring greater satisfaction to impoverished men and women than the methods of communism.

In Asia and the Middle East today, in Africa tomorrow, our ideas and practices will be more severely on trial as compared with communism than they are in Western Europe, where we have at least the advantage of familiarity with some of the traditions we inherited from and share with the Europeans. It will not be enough for us to assert faith in our own way of life, in our own ideals. It will be necessary to reinterpret that way of life, those ideals, in terms adaptable to traditions and customs completely removed from our experience.

9
REWRITING AMERICA'S PROMISES

EVER since the first explorers and pilgrims came to our shores, America has been a promised land. The Statue of Liberty holding aloft its indomitable torch has symbolized to all the world hopes for freedom, progress, prosperity. "America was promises," said the poet Archibald MacLeish.

Over the years, despite setbacks and disillusionments, these hopes have to a remarkable extent been fulfilled by immigrants who came here from all corners of the earth and joined in building a great society which found room for their diverse traditions and talents, yet left on all of them, even the most recent arrivals, the distinctive imprint of a new nation — the American nation.

Now that the United States, emerging from nearly two centuries of absorption in its own affairs, has irrevocably assumed its role as a member of the international community, we have a natural and commendable impulse to extend the promises which once beckoned those who sought a haven in the New World to all the inhabitants of the Old who are not opposed to our ideas and practices. It has not taken us long to discover, however, that the task of fulfilling promises within our borders is far simpler and more manageable than that of extending them to the rest of the non-communist world. We do not command abroad the political authority we have at home. We do not have the possibility, in other countries, of swaying votes, building up party alignments, influencing public opinion, directly affecting the press and radio, which are open to us here. True, we have at our disposal a most powerful instrument — our position as the mightiest financial and trading country of the twentieth century — which we can use with life and death effects on the economies of weaker nations.

But economic power, as we have also discovered, has its limitations. There is a point beyond which no nation, no matter how dependent it may be on our material support, will go if it has reason to believe that further concessions on its part will constitute a derogation of its political independence or will cause such deterioration in its economy as to endanger its social stability. Nor are we in a position to force on other countries internal changes which might enable them to utilize our aid more effectively, whether for their own welfare or for the security we are jointly seeking to achieve. Unless we resort to dictatorial methods, thereby belying one of America's basic promises — that of protecting the integrity and independence of all nations — we must rely on the less direct, more subtle, and far slower methods of diplomacy with which, owing to the newness of our role as a world power, we have as yet only limited experience. For us who have been brought up to make quick decisions, to reach cut-and-dried deals across the table, to work rapidly, overcoming all obstacles, to argue heatedly, sometimes vituperatively, with each other in public, the delicate and difficult art of complex negotiations with many peoples, of whom we still have only a sketchy knowledge, presents new and often sorely trying tasks. Some of our representatives, particularly those summoned to public office from private occupations and unaccustomed to international dealings, have been inclined to believe that the Russians alone are tough and inflexible negotiators who invariably wear out the patience of their American opposite numbers. Candor, however, would compel us ultimately to admit that we have not always found it easy to negotiate with the British, French, or Germans, or with the non-communist diplomats of Asia and the Middle East.

In the course of our far-flung postwar negotiations, from Greece to Japan, from France to India, we have begun to discern that America's promises cannot be thrust indiscriminately on other countries, and that some of these promises, even if they could be fulfilled, might do more harm than good to the beneficiaries of our generosity unless they have been carefully prepared in advance for such fulfillment. Of what avail is it to promise radios, television sets, washing machines, refrigerators, to people who do not yet have electricity? How helpful is it to hold out the prospect of free elections, or orate about freedom of the press, to people who cannot read and write? How efficient is it to ship tractors to people who have not been trained to use machinery, for operation on soil which may suffer rather than benefit from their use, when perhaps slightly improved customary tools might increase agricultural production? How realistic is it to urge fundamental economic and social reforms in other countries if we are not prepared to accept the possible revolutionary political consequences of our proposals?

Nor should we expect, in return for whatever we undertake to do for other nations, that they will feel ardent love or undying gratitude toward the United States. There is altogether too much preoccupation among us with the question of whether or not the Indians or French, the Russians or Chinese, "like us" or would come to "like us" if we just changed our policies. Is love really necessary, or possible, among nations? How can it be that the citizens of the greatest power in the world are so sensitive to every word of criticism uttered about them abroad? Is it possible that the superbly confident manner with which we approach the outside world — the manner of "we know best, just leave it to us" — is but a façade concealing inner incertitude and anxiety? Do we feel that the world is less our oyster than we are apt to assert? Do we have some dark if unexpressed foreboding that perhaps the way in which we are accustomed to live may not, after all, be the perfect answer to the problems of other people and that, in order to live with these others in the same world community, we must make adjustments of our own which we may not find palatable?

The simplest explanation, probably, and the one which corresponds most closely to the American character, is that we would like to be on good terms with all "strangers," and begin to feel uneasy when our slap on the back and our "hail fellow, well met" greeting are not promptly reciprocated. There is good sense in the musical comedy, *Call Me Madam*, in which Ethel Merman, as a gusty American ambassadress to a mythical duchy in Europe, offers a loan to the Foreign Minister and, when he politely declines, exclaims: "But this is an unfriendly gesture!" We *want* to be friends with other peoples. We *want* to offer them things and feel the pleasant glow of their gratitude. We might even be happy not to have them pay us back when we lend them money, provided they indicate in some concrete way their appreciation of our generosity.

This attitude of ours was wryly described by the distinguished British economist, John Maynard Keynes who, in his book *A Revision of the Treaty*, wrote in 1922:

"The average American, I fancy, would like to see the European nations approaching him with a pathetic light in their eyes and the cash in their hands saying: 'America, we owe to you our liberty and our life; here we bring what we can in grateful thanks, money not wrung by grievous taxation from the widow and orphan, but saved, the best fruits of victory, out of the abolition of armaments, militarism, Empire, and internal strife, made possible by the help you freely gave us.' And then the average American would reply: 'I honour you for your integrity. It is what I expected. But I did not enter the war for profit or to invest my money well. I have had my reward in the words you have just uttered. The loans are forgiven. Return to your homes and use the resources I release to uplift the poor and the unfortunate.' And it would be an essential part of the little scene that his reply should come as a complete and overwhelming surprise.

"Alas for the wickedness of the world! It is not in international affairs that we can secure the sentimental satisfactions which we all love. For only individuals are good, and all nations are dishonourable, cruel and designing."

Actually, there should be no worry on our part about other peoples' appreciation of our generosity. The value of our unstinted aid in a period when many nations have been recovering from the material disasters of war and others have been trying to emerge from economic backwardness, is too widely recognized to cause us any qualms. But it is not enough to give money and goods, no matter how generously. Our own preoccupation with material satisfaction as an essential ingredient of happiness, and our belief that material achievement is of utmost, perhaps paramount, importance in determining the degree of progress attained by other nations, make us believe that the best aid we can give to less fortunate peoples is in terms of goods and dollars. Yet material gifts, especially when distributed by a nation which constantly boasts of its stupendous power to produce an unlimited amount, are least likely to bring affection in return. The giver is bound to show some sort of satisfaction with his generosity, whether expressed in an ostentatious manner or in a manner of obviously unnatural modesty. The recipient is bound to feel an object of charity, so that the milk of human gratitude within him turns to poison. When the Lady Bountiful of English novels used to go about among the tenantry, bringing calves'-foot jelly into their hovels, the gift may have been welcome; but it also served to emphasize the vast, then unbridgeable, gap separating the manor from the lowly cottage.

What promises, then, can we make with some expectation that they will be fulfilled? Let us discuss them under six main headings:

1. *Political Democracy*. We cannot promise to establish in other countries political institutions modeled on those of the United States. No amount of exertion, skill, and expenditure on our part can duplicate in countries unfamiliar with the experience we ourselves inherited from England and, in a larger context, from Western civilization in general, the conditions that proved peculiarly favorable to the development of political democracy in the United States. When we have tried to do this, even under circumstances over which we had most control, as in postwar Germany and Japan, we have discovered that while we can give other peoples the *forms*, the outer trappings and rituals, of democracy, we cannot give them the *content*. This they alone can develop if they want to — and that is a fundamental "if." We cannot start revolutions in other countries. What we can do is not oppose leaders who are endeavoring to reform conditions that we ourselves recognize to be obsolete and oppressive. If we decide to promote actively the "liberation" of Russia's satellites in Eastern Europe, we must realize that we shall have to promise not only freedom from Soviet rule but also political democracy, a modernized economy, and security against encroachments by a reunited and rearmed Germany.

We can promise that if other peoples are willing to go through an experience comparable to our own — if over a considerable period of years they are willing to assume opportunities for universal public education, the protection of political and other minorities, the untrammeled formation of more than one party, the encouragement of a sense of public service — we shall do everything within our power to help them make the best of such opportunities. We can offer to share the experience of our businessmen, our labor leaders, our teachers, our social workers, and others in our communities who are engaged in the multiform tasks of fostering democracy. But it is *they* who must decide that they want political changes in the direction of democracy and who must shape to their own ends such lessons as they wish to learn from us. Nor should we feel that a decision by another nation not to copy our institutions represents a slur on the American way of life.

2. *Economic and Social Institutions.* We cannot promise to establish in other countries an economic and social system modeled on that of the United States in the same way as an American businessman may promise to set up in India or Brazil an industrial plant modeled on his own. Human institutions are not factories. Our economic and social institutions, like our political democracy, are the product of conditions peculiar to this country, conditions that are in many respects unique and cannot be reproduced elsewhere with machinelike precision. As Keith Funston, president of the New York Stock Exchange, has pointed out, "American capitalism is as American as apple pie." We cannot merely transfer American capitalism to countries which either have allowed their capitalism to fall into desuetude, as in Europe, or have never experienced it, as in Asia, the Middle East, and Latin America. Nor is anything gained if we disguise the inability of other nations to duplicate our production and distribution standards by grants or subsidies which may merely postpone necessary internal transformations.

We can promise that if other countries are willing to strengthen their economies by various means — land reforms, abolition of production and distribution cartels and labor restrictions, overhaul of obsolete taxation systems, eradication of illiteracy, improved conditions of rural credit, road building and sanitation, introduction of electricity, and a dozen other measures fitted to their particular requirements — we shall help them to the extent of our ability. We can also promise not to assert, on grounds of military necessity, prior claims to the strategic raw materials they produce and may need for their own economic modernization and development.

We can promise that if they agree to give reasonable protection to the investments of our private investors, on terms no less favorable — but not more favorable — than those given to the private investors of other nations, we in our turn shall not demand that their governments accept our concept of competitive enterprise. We can promise not to block, directly or indirectly, whatever measures they regard as necessary for the transformation of obsolete or backward economies into modern systems, even if this should involve the introduction in one form or another of what we call socialism. We can promise that if other countries make an effort to improve their internal economic conditions, we shall endeavor to facilitate their exports to the United States as well as to other world markets and shall not discourage or prevent these exports out of deference to some of our own domestic producers, as Congress has done, for example, by restricting the importation into this country of cheeses produced by friendly nations — Canada, the Netherlands, France, Denmark, and Italy.

This is not a revolutionary program. Those of our businessmen who have had experience in Western Europe and Asia during the postwar years clearly see that mutual accommodation of diverse economic and social systems, rather than the imposition of the American system on other nations, is the most likely prospect for the future. They do not regard it as either practicable or desirable to have the United States become a mere source of handouts to countries facing economic difficulties. In their opinion the governments of countries which want to absorb American aid effectively will have voluntarily to make fundamental changes in their own tax and production structure, even if this does mean disturbance of capitalist, as well as labor, interests. And they urge the American public to recognize the sadly neglected fact that we cannot have exports unless we are much more willing than we have been in the past to increase our imports.

Nor is it any longer as difficult for us as it once was to live in friendship, or at least without mutual recrimination, side by side with nations whose economic and social institutions differ from our own. After years first of bitter criticism, then of resigned headshaking and viewing with alarm about British socialism, we have come to accept it as a feature of the world landscape, and we have even begun to understand that the British Conservatives, confronted by the country's long-term deep-seated problems, would be unable, and are in any case not ready, to discard the principal changes effected by the Labor government. Nor have many Americans balked at Washington's policy of doing business with totalitarian Franco Spain and with communist-ruled Yugoslavia.

3. *Americans and Reforms.* We cannot move into other countries, like a cleanup squad, to effect such internal changes as we think might be of direct benefit to them, and of indirect benefit to us. If we do so, no matter how pure our intentions, we shall promptly be accused, and not only by Communists but most vehemently also by conservative nationalists, of unjustifiable interference in other countries' affairs, of "imperialism" and "dictatorship."

We can undertake to view with sympathy efforts made in other countries to bring about reforms, even if these reforms also have the support of Communists, as they often do. For example, when directly confronted with the problem, we have recognized the necessity of carrying out land reforms in Japan and South Korea, even though we realize that land reform alone, if unaccompanied by literacy, agrarian mechanization, the development of light industries, and other measures, will not solve the problems of underdeveloped nations.

Land reform is not revolutionary. In 1951 the United States, after having for years left the propaganda initiative in this sphere to the U.S.S.R., introduced a sweeping land-reform program in the United Nations Economic and Social Council. Washington hopes that this program can be carried out without the forced collectivization and political dictatorship which have marked land reform in Russia, Eastern Europe, and communist China. In South Korea, once a truce has been concluded, the United States will have the signal opportunity of completing the kind of land reform it considers practicable under democratic conditions. Americans familiar with Korean problems urge that to eliminate any possible accusation of American imperialism, such a program should be sponsored by the United Nations.

4. *Relations with Labor.* We cannot move into other countries to check the abuses of a belated or arrested Industrial Revolution and to improve relations between employers and workers. Since we ourselves are still divided — as foreign visitors are quick to note — about the role labor should play in modern society, intervention by the United States in the industrial affairs of other nations might cause more harm than good.

We can undertake to view the interests of labor in other countries with at least as much sympathy as the interests of employers. We can use our influence to persuade industrialists and bankers in countries to which we are giving financial aid that it is to their own advantage — as it has proved to the advantage of our most enlightened industrialists and bankers here — to give workers an increasing opportunity to share in the fruits of expanded production and thereby acquire a stake in the well-being of their nation's economy which would act as a safeguard against the pressures of communism.

Our industrial and financial leaders, who believe in the flexibility and further potential growth of democratic capitalism, could constitute themselves a new corps of economic diplomats.

They could persuade their opposite numbers in other countries that increased productivity, permitting the output of more goods at lower prices, would bring within the reach of workers consumer goods, better housing, improved school, hospital, and other community services which today represent the core of the American worker's high living standard. American labor leaders have shown the way by telling labor leaders of other continents that although they are by no means entirely satisfied with existing conditions in the United States — who ever is? — they intend to bring about improvement by peaceful negotiation with employers rather than by resort to class war and totalitarian methods.

This, also, is not a revolutionary program. The need for it has been recognized by so realistic a capitalist statesman as Bernard Baruch who, in an interview with Marguerite Higgins published in the *New York Herald Tribune* of August 15, 1951, said: "The masses everywhere are on the trek and cannot be stopped, for the common man has learned that he is essential to modern total war. The democracies must turn their backs on the era when the masses were exploited and downtrodden. It must be our crusade to get the masses on our side everywhere in the world."

5. *How Much Armament?* We cannot promise to take upon ourselves the task of defending by force of arms all countries which feel menaced by Russia and/or communism. If we tried to carry out such a promise, the United States would have to assume political obligations and military burdens far in excess of those borne by Britain in the heyday of its empire. In the Victorian age several other great powers were in existence and proved capable of helping to maintain a balance of power, not only in Europe but in other parts of the world as well. The United States does not need to assume the role of residuary legatee of all previous great powers and their colonial empires with the exception of Russia and communist China. Now that

other nations, both our former allies and our former enemies, are recovering from the aftermath of World War II, they will become increasingly capable of assuming their share of whatever armament obligations we jointly decide are necessary to check Russia and communism. Now that Russia can also produce the atomic bomb, no matter how crudely, this apocalyptic weapon has become a double-edged threat, and we must persist in seeking to achieve international controls over all armaments — both "conventional" and "unconventional." Above all we must assure other nations that we shall not recklessly make gestures or utter threats that might precipitate war.

We can promise to give help against aggression by Russia or any other great power, as well as against subversion by communism or other totalitarian movements, to any country which desires to defend itself. We must not look upon the armed forces of any nation as mercenaries whom we shall furnish with arms and other war materials, thereby conserving our own manpower, but as teammates in the tasks of collective security, jointly sharing with us the hardships, sacrifices, and safeguards. We must not expect them to fight or to man bases solely for our sake, any more than we help them solely for their own sake. But we can expect them to fight for the sake of maintaining a collective-security system under the sponsorship of the United Nations, which they would regard as a form of insurance for themselves as well as for us.

This, again, is not a revolutionary program. We have already inaugurated it through our historic decision of June 25, 1950, to embark on the Korean War not as a national undertaking but to place our armed forces, which constitute the bulk of the forces engaged in Korea, at the disposal of the United Nations. We can follow the example we ourselves set in Korea by similarly fitting the European army, which SHAPE is in the process of forging out of the national armies of the North Atlantic Treaty Organization members, within the United

Nations framework. We would thereby take a great step forward from the national armies and the temporary coalitions of the past toward the international force, dedicated to defense of the world community against aggression from any quarter, that the builders of the League of Nations and the UN have regarded as an essential feature of an effective international organization.

6. *Underdeveloped Lands.* We cannot promise to rehabilitate and develop, singlehandedly, the economies of all underdeveloped lands opposed to Russia — least of all if we should insist that uncompromising opposition to Russia and unquestioning acquiescence in all our policies must be an essential precondition of our aid, as some of our Congressmen urged in 1951 when aid for India was under discussion. There is a powerful appeal for us in the prospect that the United States, which has proved so successful in developing the American continent, might now set forth to apply its pioneering spirit and technological experience to Asia, the Middle East, Africa, and Latin America. This would be the realization of a dream nurtured by some among us — the dream of "The American Century," with a benevolent United States shouldering a new "white man's burden" and conferring the benefits of the American way of life on backward peoples.

But not only would the realization of this dream entail expenditures which Congress hitherto has been unwilling to envisage. It has also become abundantly clear from the experience of the postwar years that other countries, no matter how much they admire American democracy and hope to benefit by the lessons of our technology, are by no means prepared to become mere carbon copies of the American system. They want to be free to choose whatever economic and social practices seem best adapted to their needs and traditions, and to use those technical experts — not necessarily always American — whose particular knowledge seems most valuable at their given stage of agricultural and industrial development.

We can promise to give such aid as we believe to be within our capacity to leaders of underdeveloped areas who are ready to introduce political, economic, and social reforms which would make our aid useful to their peoples. At the same time, to avoid the possibility that the grant of American aid might be attacked as "imperialism" and "intervention," we would be well advised to channel as much of our assistance as possible through the United Nations and its affiliated international agencies like the Food and Agriculture Organization and the World Health Organization.

In short, America's promises to the rest of the world need to be rewritten, not in the language of old-fashioned nationalism or a "take it or leave it" policy, but in terms of twentieth-century international cooperation based on the interlocking concepts of self-help and mutual aid. It is tempting for a great power to play the role of *deus ex machina* and brush aside the counsel of weaker nations for the sake of what it regards as "the larger end" — all too often identifying its own national interests with what it quite honestly conceives to be the interests of the universe. We shall constantly have to be on guard against this temptation.

Our main preoccupation in the next fifty years will not be to discover how we can transpose our way of life to other continents, by force, diplomacy, or financial inducement, but how we can fuse the civilization developed here with other civilizations of the world in such a way as to strengthen the fabric of international society. The variegated interests of men transcend the boundaries of nation-states. In the battle of ideas we shall not succeed if we plead for universal allegiance to the American idea, which can no more encompass the universe than the Russian, British, German, French, or Indian idea. At issue today is not the need for international cooperation, but its degree at any given time and in any given place.

If we are to make friends for the United States, we must learn to understand and get along with other peoples — not merely expect them to understand and get along with us. We must be careful not to adopt a fundamentalist policy of perfectionism. We must not demand unconditional surrender and abject acquiescence. To the making of foreign policy we must bring our traditional skill for experimentation. "The spirit of liberty," says Justice Learned Hand, "is the spirit which is not too sure that it is right."

To succeed, we must remedy two of our national shortcomings. An impatient people, we must acquire an infinite fund of patience. A nation with a brief history, hitherto remarkably free from setbacks, we must acquire a sense of historical perspective. But we have one great asset which should serve us well — our still lively belief in the perfectibility of man. This belief, provided we avoid the pitfalls of dogmatism, could rekindle the hopes of ancient nations, worn by age-long struggles. On this belief we are wagering our own destiny and that of the rest of the world.

We must also learn that morality and power are not necessarily irreconcilable. Power, as such, whether of armaments or money, is neither good nor evil. What can be good or evil is the use we make of our power. There has been a recent tendency among us, as we began, in our new role, to acquire the rudiments of *realpolitik*, to assume that power must be divorced from morality. Yet in the past our strength has been due far more to our moral principles than to our physical resources or weapons. What we must beware of is not morality, but our frequent desire to moralize about world events, without assuming the responsibility for implementing the moral principles we proclaim and which, if implemented, could have a richly fructifying effect on the world community.

IO

INGREDIENTS OF A
FEARLESS POLICY

WHEN Gen. Dwight D. Eisenhower, in a landslide victory on November 4, 1952, received an unprecedented popular mandate for the presidency of the United States, it became his destiny to take over the conduct of foreign policy in a country which in the brief span of less than fifteen years had moved from the "neutralism" of the pre-1939 period to the global interventionism and wide-ranging international cooperation of the 1950s. His nomination at the Republican party convention in Chicago over Senator Robert A. Taft, the "Mr. Republican" who had become a symbol of surviving isolationist sentiment, was universally interpreted as a final rejection by the party he chose to lead of the isolationism that in 1919, in the hands of Senator Henry Cabot Lodge and others, had wrecked the hopes of a Democratic president, Woodrow Wilson, for American participation in the League of Nations.

While Republican spokesmen, both during the presidential campaign and after their candidate's sweeping personal victory, bitterly attacked various features of the Democratic Administration's foreign policy, contending that it was "time for a change," they at the same time assured the country that no reversal of the new role of world leadership assumed by the United States after 1945 was under contemplation. Since President Eisenhower ran way ahead of his party in the elections, he is in an unexcelled position to determine the objectives and implementation not only of foreign policy but also of the domestic policy which it necessarily reflects. Unless he succumbs to the opposition of Senators and Representatives who have hitherto stood for isolation abroad and reactionary practices at home, he should be able to give an impressive demonstration of his often expressed conviction that the Republicans can carry out far more effectively than the Democrats international commitments in whose formulation and fulfillment many of their liberal spokesmen had taken part in the past decade.

President Eisenhower, moreover, will have a significant advantage over President Truman. For even if he does not succeed in inducing the Jenners, the Bridges, and the other Republican die-hards to alter their views on world affairs, he can count not only on the support of his more enlightened followers but also on that of Republican-oriented Dixiecrats who, representing a traditionally internationalist region of the country, will now have the additional inducement of enlarging the newly initiated Republican inroads into the Solid South. Nor is it possible to believe that the Democrats above the Mason and Dixon line who propelled a dynamic international policy into existence will permit partisan considerations to erode the record of achievement chalked up by Woodrow Wilson, Franklin D. Roosevelt, and Harry S. Truman, and clarified during the presidential campaign by Adlai Stevenson.

Assuming, then, that the elements of the Republican party now in power will hold firm to the principle of international cooperation, the question to be answered in the next four years becomes not, "Will the Republicans continue the foreign policy of the Democrats?" but "What will the Republicans do differently from the Democrats?"

In answering this question, it must be recognized, in all

candor, that — irrespective of party — any new administration would have found it necessary to make a thoroughgoing review of this country's foreign policy. The past decade of war and cold war has been crowded with tumultuous events and critical decisions taken in emergency situations each of which seemed or was claimed to spell catastrophe. It would have been a miracle — and miracles seldom attend the affairs of men — if all these decisions had proved wise, especially when subjected to the disillusioning test of hindsight speculation. It would have been a miracle, also, if all the new institutions hastily erected to deal with unfamiliar situations had turned out to have been solidly built on the rock of time. Human events are never static. The United States itself has undergone far-reaching changes since 1941. Europe is moving from the stage of dependent convalescence to that of assertive independence. Asia, the Middle East, Africa, Latin America are astir with nationalism which often finds expression in anti-Westernism. The U.S.S.R. cannot be counted on to stand still.

The Republican Administration, no matter how far it expects to go with its plans for a "cleanup" of the men and agencies hitherto charged with administering foreign policy, will find that it cannot reverse certain decisions or discard certain institutions. It can prune away dead wood, tighten up machinery here and there, replace Democrats with Republicans in key offices. It can, and doubtless will want to, consolidate the position attained by the United States in world affairs under a policy which, in large part, enjoyed bipartisan support, notably during the life of Senator Arthur H. Vandenberg of Michigan. But unless the Republicans suddenly decide to raze the whole structure of foreign policy, they cannot move back. For them only one course is open — to move forward.

But forward to what? Forward to a policy of increasing cooperation with other nations which would give sympathetic consideration to their trade problems, their national aspira-

tions, their racial difficulties, their hopes and fears? Or forward
to a policy based on the assumption that the United States,
with its seemingly limitless capacity for production, its technological ability to out-produce Russia not only in peacetime
goods but also in the implements of war — including the
atomic and hydrogen bomb — its financial resources superior
to those of any country in the world, can tell other countries
what to do, can arbitrarily mold their destiny to harmonize
with its own?

This is the Gethsemane faced by every great power, every
great movement, in history: whether it is better to grasp the
visible attributes of power and lose the world, or let them pass
by and gain the essence of moral authority. The Democrats,
now cast for the first time in twenty years in the role of loyal
opposition, cannot avoid some part of the responsibility for this
agonizing choice. But the ultimate responsibility for the direction in which the United States moves during the next four
years will rest on the Republicans.

Their task will be complicated in one significant respect.
Their own utterances — in the period when, condemned to
the political wilderness, they denounced every Democratic policy in season and out — have created the impression abroad
that, with a few notable exceptions, the Republicans are conservatives, if not reactionaries, in a world that is passing through
one of the great revolutions of history. Their much-publicized
opposition to the emergence of labor on the national scene,
their bitter attacks on social welfare measures as "creeping socialism," and, more recently during the campaign, the efforts
of Republican spokesmen, notably President Eisenhower himself, to placate the leaders of "white supremacy" in the South,
including James F. Byrnes of South Carolina and Herman
Talmadge of Georgia, have raised many doubts among non-
Communists outside the United States about the kind of ideas
the Republicans may be expected to pour into the already

accepted molds of international action. Nor were the early prognostications of future policy by organs of the press favorable to the Republicans encouraging in this respect. *The U.S. News and World Report,* for example, in predicting the outlook of the new Administration shortly after the election, declared with profound satisfaction that "ideals are out" and that henceforth the course of the United States in world affairs would be dictated by hard-boiled practical considerations of national interest.

Yet the new Secretary of State, John Foster Dulles, in a series of pronouncements preceding the election of Eisenhower, berated the Democratic Administration for its alleged failure to proclaim "positive" ideas and asserted his belief that the world-wide struggle against Russia and communism could be won more effectively by moral principles than by guns and bombs. It is therefore premature to jump to the conclusion that in deference to the concepts of hard-boiled realism the Republican Administration will formulate foreign policy solely in terms of dollars and cents, or regard expediency as the only determinant of this country's relations with other nations.

Nor is it fair to assume, or let our friends abroad assume, that anti-labor or anti-Negro sentiment is restricted to Republicans. The Byrneses and Talmadges, for better or worse, have until now belonged to the Democratic fold. If the Republicans can boast of Joseph R. McCarthy of Wisconsin and his irresponsible witch hunts, the Democrats can match him any time with Pat McCarran of Nevada and his ill-famed immigration and naturalization law. Neither party is free of obscurantist elements, and each has it within its capacity to rise above them. It is probably closer to the truth to say, as a British writer, Raymond English, put it in the autumn 1952 issue of *The American Scholar,* that "although Americans think and talk of themselves as Liberals, they tend to act and subconsciously believe as Conservatives."

If that is the case — and no one except a reactionary fanatic would accuse ex-President Truman or Dean Acheson of being a radical — the ultimate difference between Democrats and Republicans in the administration of foreign policy, distressing though this may seem to the minority of our staunchest liberals, may prove to be a difference not so much of essence as of degree.

How would this difference of degree affect Washington's decisions on the eight major issues which face the new Administration?

(1) By promising during the campaign to make a personal on-the-spot study of the situation in *Korea*, Eisenhower placed the stalemated Korean War at the top of his international agenda. No responsible American, even in the heat of campaigning, expected that Eisenhower singlehanded could by some stroke of pen or sword cut the Gordian knot of the complex Asian crisis of which Korea is but one, if at the moment for us the most agonizing, aspect. Eisenhower's cautious statements on his return from a three-day visit to Korea made clear that he did not expect to produce a magic formula for termination of the conflict. His plans, apparently, then included such measures as expansion of the South Korean forces, improvements in the supply of armaments, and increased pressures on the Communist armies, of which the decision to lift restrictions on Chinese Nationalist raids from Formosa was the first overt move. Talk was heard that the United States would insist on a stringent naval blockade of communist China, and might consider the use of Chiang Kai-shek's Nationalist soldiers on the Korean front. There was no indication, however, that the President or Secretary of State Dulles were contemplating extension of the war to the China mainland or resort to atomic or hydrogen bombs in Korea.

No matter how much additional military pressure the Republican Administration may bring to bear against the communist forces on the Korean battlefield, it is doubtful that a settlement can be reached in Korea until and unless the United States is ready to consider discussion of the other issues in dispute between the West and Russia in Asia. Among these issues are recognition of the communist regime in China and its admission to the United Nations; the future military and economic role of Japan, which twice since 1890 has invaded China, and once in this century, in 1904–1905, inflicted a disastrous defeat on Czarist Russia; and the retention by Britain and France of their remaining footholds on Asian soil, Malaya and Indo-China. These issues are rightly considered to be of vital interest to the United States. But they are also of vital interest to Russia and China, and have been since the turn of the century — not only on the ideological ground of communism, as often assumed in this country, but also on strategic and economic grounds which would be of concern to the two powers even if non-communist governments should rule in Moscow and Peiping.

The Democrats, walking a perilous tightrope on China policy, avoided the two possible extremes — recognition of Peiping, which under their administration would have been denounced by the Republicans as "appeasement," and extension of the war through the dispatch of Chiang Kai-shek's Formosa troops to Korea, the bombing of Manchuria, or the use of Japanese manpower — all of which have at various times been advocated by some Republican spokesmen. The Republicans can, to some extent, improve the strategic position of the United Nations in Korea by consolidating the various policies the Democrats had initiated in Asia. They can recognize, as the NATO Council at its last session with Mr. Acheson in December 1952, recognized, that France's struggle against the Vietminh in Indo-China is an integral part of the defense of Asia against communism, and perhaps shoulder a larger share of the financial and armament burden hitherto borne by the

French — although this will mean more, instead of less, expenditures on foreign aid. They can press forward with the organization of the Pacific defense coalition, and perhaps accede to Britain's demand for a role in this coalition, although the accretion of strength gained thereby would be moral rather than material, and thus might not satisfy the hard-boiled school of thought in Republican ranks. They can continue to pretend, as the Democrats did under Republican pressure, that the Chinese Communists, who admittedly control the territory of mainland China, are really not there — even though the United States, on behalf of the United Nations, has been negotiating with Chinese Communist representatives at Panmunjom. They can insist that the Japanese accelerate their rearmament, and even weigh the possibility of using Japanese forces in Korea.

None of these courses, however, either alone or taken together, would bring the Korean War to an end unless Russia and China are satisfied that their national interests, illegitimate though these seem to us, will be protected by an all-Asian, or at least a Far Eastern, settlement. If the Republicans want to bring the war in Korea to an early close, they will either have to discuss other Asian problems as well with Russia and China, thereby at least tacitly admitting the existence of a communist regime in Peiping; or else they will have to consider the possibility of extending the war to China and, if necessary, to Russia, in the hope of breaking the Korean stalemate by force. An enlarged conflict in Asia, which might portend a third world war, would hardly seem consonant with the optimistic views on peace and prosperity voiced by the spokesmen of American business who, except for the Secretary of Labor, are in complete control of the Eisenhower cabinet. The theory popular after World War I that wars are caused by industrialists and bankers has been pretty well exploded. A full-scale war would hardly be conducive to the cuts in government expenditures, reductions in taxes, or the genuine abandonment of government controls, all of which are important features of the Republicans' domestic program. While some of our friends in Europe and Asia have expressed anxiety about the possibly warlike intentions of a military man as president, it may be expected that Eisenhower, more effectively than if he were a civilian, would be in a position to curb war-minded military officials. His Secretary of State, moreover, is well known for his great reluctance, in 1939, to contemplate war with nazi Germany, and there is no reason to expect that he would view war with Russia with greater enthusiasm, although his campaign statements about the "liberation" of Eastern Europe were interpreted in London, Paris, and Bonn as an invitation for armed attack on Russia's satellites and, through them, on the Kremlin.

It is interesting, in this connection, to note that Joseph C. Grew, a veteran diplomat, in his memoirs, *Turbulent Era*, has recorded his criticisms of the Roosevelt Administration for not exploring, up until Pearl Harbor, all possible avenues to a peaceful settlement with Japan, which in the 1940s was regarded as no less a menace to the United States than Russia is regarded today. Discussing "the futility of war," Mr. Grew declares: "Any unnecessary war, whether it be won or lost, must be averted if humanly possible." He then goes on to say: "So long as any nation follows policies designed exclusively for the protection and furtherance of its own interests and is not solicitous to assist in resolving the problems of other nations whose well-being is equally necessary for the operation of a world economy such as we have today, just so long will the progress of civilization and the welfare of mankind be retarded through unnecessary and futile wars."

Should the Eisenhower Administration follow the kind of advice which Mr. Grew feels he vainly proffered to Franklin D. Roosevelt in 1941, and stand ready to explore any possibility of negotiation with Stalin — as Mr. Dulles indicated he would when commenting on Stalin's answers to the questions posed by James Reston at Christmas 1952 — it would enjoy one decisive advantage over the Democrats: for no one outside the lunatic fringe of professional anti-Communists could possibly accuse a Republican cabinet of being "soft" toward communism. If the Korean War is to be brought to an end by over-all Asian negotiations, this can be done far more successfully by the Republicans than by the Democrats.

 (2) The same thing is true of *Western Europe*. There the new Administration must reach a series of complex decisions about the future of the European Defense Community, whose creation has been increasingly threatened by renewed tension between France and Germany, due in part to France's anxiety that its involvement in Indo-China might so weaken its military and economic position in Europe as to facilitate the swift return of Germany to a role of dominance on the Continent.

Despite the election-campaign debate as to which should take precedence in our strategic plans, Europe or Asia, it is clear that the commitments of Britain and France in Malaya and Indo-China create a link between developments in the two continents which no degree of political prestidigitation can cause to disappear — unless, of course, as some leading French non-Communists have suggested, France turns over its Indo-China obligations to the United States and concentrates its attention on Europe. Even then, however, it must be expected that the Germans, with a technological "know-how" and a willingness to work unmatched in Europe, will again emerge as the leading nation on the Continent. No amount of anxiety on the part of the French can exorcise this reality. This will prove particularly true if the German people, not content with the integration of West Germany into the European community, continue to insist on the reunification of West and East Germany, which is increasingly urged by such non-communist groups as the Social Democratic party and the Protestant Church.

The Democratic Administration tried to reconcile the interests of France and West Germany, and believed they had done so through the device of the European army first proposed by the French and subsequently supported by Eisenhower when he was commander-in-chief of the NATO forces. But the Democrats, almost as fearful of the word "socialism" as the Republicans, were never able to establish a harmonious working relationship with the German Social Democrats, except in beleaguered Berlin, and hoped against hope that German unity could be indefinitely postponed until West Germany, under a conservative government presumably friendly to the United States, had been firmly meshed into the Western coalition.

If this coalition should now be threatened, or at least postponed, by French fears of German resurgence and German insistence on unity ahead of rearmament, the Republican Administration will face two possible alternatives. Either it will have to rely on a bilateral alliance with Germany — as urged by some American military observers — at the risk of antagonizing France, which might then return to the policy it has followed since the 1890s of seeking the aid of Russia against a united Germany (such a course has been favored by General de Gaulle); or it will have to strengthen France in Europe as well as in Indo-China, at the risk that West Germany will seek unity through negotiations with Russia, and then drift away from the Western coalition. In either case the Republicans, no matter how great their repugnance toward "socialism," will have to deal with the German Social Democrats if they are to avoid the possibility, on the one hand, of resurgent nazism in West Germany, or of an outright "deal" between a conservative government in Bonn and the Kremlin by which the Germans would recover their lost territories in the East and gain access to the markets of Russia and China, while Russia and China would obtain from the Ruhr the steel and machinery needed for their further industrialization.

Given the opposition to rearmament of a large segment of the German people, the Republican Administration would find it difficult to impose rearmament on the Germans without stultifying the moral principles proclaimed by Mr. Dulles — unless Eisenhower is prepared to rely on the support of the extreme Rightist elements which want the establishment of a national German army, and might conceivably force their concept on the German people if aided in this project by the United States. The extreme Rightists, however, are outspokenly anti-American, and could hardly be expected to back the United States except for as long as it would take them to recreate a German force which could then be used to recapture the territories Germany lost to Russia and Poland at the close of World War II. If, however, as assumed here, a general war is not on the agenda of the Republican Administration, this approach to the problem of German rearmament would hardly appear tempting. Nor would it be long possible for the Republican Administration to proclaim that the United States is the leader of a democratic coalition if the armed aid of West Germany could be obtained only at the hands of men dedicated to totalitarianism.

Under these circumstances it would seem wiser for the Republicans, again in line with Mr. Grew's formula that wars are futile and that no stone should be left unturned for the sake of negotiations, to explore every possible avenue of discussing with the U.S.S.R. the possibility of a peaceful reunification of Germany, even if such reunification were to be accompanied by a pledge that the Germans, for the time being, would remain demilitarized. True, such a settlement, if attainable, would require the continuance of American military aid to Western Europe, and this might be regarded by economy-minded Republicans as undesirable. But if it comes

to a choice of evils, the evil of allocating more American manpower and armaments to Western Europe would seem less
than the evil of restoring German militarism, over which we
would then have no control, and creating a situation where
Russia would be able to claim it was being menaced by German remilitarization — and would have many willing listeners
among Western Europeans who have not forgotten the cruelties and depredations of nazi conquest. What is said here about
the rearmament of Germany applies with equal force to that
of Japan, whose conquest of south Asia is also fresh in the
memories of its victims.

(3) Closely linked to the fate of the European Defense
Community is the problem faced by the Republican Administration in reconciling its campaign denunciation of "containment" and its pledge to *"liberate" Eastern Europe* with its
promise to cut taxes and to whittle down defense expenditures.

The Democrats had believed that "containment" might
eventually bring about either the disintegration of the Soviet
system or a more conciliatory attitude on the part of the
Kremlin, without the need of risking the disastrous consequences of a third world war. If the Republican Administration
acts on the belief that "containment" is not enough, and should
be replaced by a more dynamic policy, it might have to seek
the aid of the Germans in putting pressure on Russia, with or
without a resort to outright military action. If the Republicans
did so, they would again enhance the position of Germany in
Europe at the risk of alienating not only France, but also the
peoples of the countries it wants to liberate — Poles, Czechs,
and Hungarians — who were conquered by the Nazis before
they were subjugated by the Russians. Such a policy, instead
of leading to liberation, might have the opposite effect of
decimating the anti-communist forces in the satellite countries
and consolidating Russia's rule. Moreover, if the Republicans
should use Germany to liberate Eastern Europe, they would

have to accept what the Democrats have hitherto been reluctant to face — the reunification of East and West Germany.
For only after the Eastern zone of Germany has been freed
from the Russians would it be possible for the Western powers
to reach the nations of Eastern Europe directly.

Assuming, however, that the Republican Administration
foregoes the possibility of using Germany as a battering-ram
to break Russia's hold on Eastern Europe, it would still have
to present the peoples of that area with a program other than
mere return to the conditions they knew before 1939 if it is to
wean them away from Russia and win their support for the
West. In all of these countries — with the notable exception
of Czechoslovakia — dictatorship, the interlocking of Church
and State, and a semifeudal economy were common denominators in the interwar period, making them vulnerable first
to nazi propaganda and German conquest, then to communist
propaganda and Russian domination. To speak to these countries, whose conditions were in many respects similar to those
of the underdeveloped areas of the Middle East and Asia, of
"free enterprise," American democracy, and American standards of living would be as unrealistic as to speak in these terms
to Egypt or Yugoslavia. If the Republicans sincerely want to
liberate Eastern Europe, they may have to face the necessity
of accepting some form of socialism, or even communism, in
that area, so long as these countries are not controlled by Moscow and armed by it against their neighbors. The use of
American funds to encourage desertion and subversion among
Communists, often described as a "positive" policy, is merely
a negation of communism, and offers no substitute for the
promise of positive reforms.

President Eisenhower's announcement in his State of the
Union message of February 2 that Chinese Nationalist forces
on Formosa had been freed for raids against the communist
China mainland, and the visit to Western Europe of Secretary

of State John Foster Dulles, who urged the European nations to create the stalled European army by April at the latest, represent pressures on Russia and China to end the Korean War stalemate. Will these pressures bring about the desired effect? Or will they have to be followed by more extensive measures — such as American participation in Chiang Kai-shek's proposed operations on the China mainland, the immediate rearming of Japan, a free rein for Germany to recover the territories it lost in the east after World War II, by force if necessary? Are we on the eve of an era of global negotiations leading to stabilization, or on the eve of World War III?

Answers to these questions hinge on one's estimate of the real strength of the U.S.S.R., which, as the principal industrial nation in the Soviet bloc, serves as the arsenal for communist China and for the Eastern European satellites. On this point there has been considerable divergence of opinion between the United States and its Western European allies. Here the U.S.S.R. is often depicted as a "monolithic," powerful state, commanding not only decisive land force superiority but also modern weapons such as the atomic bomb and having at its disposal the ideological weapon of communist propaganda. The Western European nations, however, on the basis of their intelligence information, have expressed doubts about the internal solidity and the military sticking power, in Europe at least, of the U.S.S.R. and regard American insistence on the need for hasty rearmament and accelerated unification of Western Europe as exaggerated. And ex-President Truman, since his retirement, has said he was "not convinced" that the Russians have the atomic bomb.

This statement was promptly contradicted by President Eisenhower in his State of the Union message when he declared, "We have incontrovertible evidence that Soviet Russia possesses atomic weapons." However, according to a distinguished student of atomic problems, William L. Laurence of *The New York Times*, Mr. Truman may be right in the sense that the Russians are still in the early stages of learning how to make a successful, highly efficient bomb — and that "a man in a jalopy is no match against a driver in a de luxe 1953 model."

Whatever may be the truth about the present military strength of the U.S.S.R., which in turn will affect the military strength of communist China, evidence is accumulating that the Soviet government is genuinely and profoundly concerned over internal strains and stresses, not only at home but perhaps even more in the Eastern European satellites and particularly in East Germany. Mounting accusations against Jews are regarded by observers close to the scene less as an indication of anti-Semitism than as an hysterical anxiety that the better-informed and more thoughtful members of the Soviet bloc are being affected by Western ideas.

If the Soviet government had only Russia to deal with, the current purges, as in the 1930s, might strengthen the political leaders who come out on top. But the need to deal with Eastern European countries which in some respects are more advanced than the U.S.S.R. greatly complicates the task of the Kremlin. The powerful growth since 1945 of Russian nationalism, which operates not only against Zionists but also against non-Russian national elements within the U.S.S.R., has gravely undermined the international appeal of communism; and outside of Russia, communist influence — as distinguished from dissatisfaction with existing non-communist governments — is on the wane.

Under the circumstances some seasoned students of Russia believe that the time may be near when it will prove possible for the United States to negotiate with the U.S.S.R. with some hope of concrete results. The purges of 1953, in their opinion, signal the end, not the beginning, of a profound internal readjustment in Moscow — a readjustment which has reduced and perhaps altogether eliminated the power of the secret police and military elements who are believed to have favored strong action against the West. According to this estimate, George F. Kennan, former United States Ambassador to Moscow, found it impossible to talk with the Russians because the Kremlin, during his incumbency, was in the throes of the crisis which resulted in leadership changes, and had no intention of having its difficulties exposed to the West through the reports of so well-informed an observer as Mr. Kennan. If this appraisal is accurate, Charles F. Bohlen, who succeeded Mr. Kennan, may now find the Kremlin in a less intransigent mood.

Assuming that the purpose of United States foreign policy is still to create "situations of strength" from which the West can ultimately negotiate with Moscow, some thought might usefully be given to the minimum diplomatic objectives of the West. In Europe, will the West welcome the unification of Germany, which would alter the balance of power of the proposed European Community and European army? How will the West reconcile the desire for liberation of Eastern Europe with the rebuilding of German armed strength? If the Russians are to withdraw into their 1939 borders, what will be the future role of American and British troops on the Continent? And in Asia, does the West hope to eject the Chinese Communists from North Korea, and achieve a reunited Korea under non-communist auspices? Does it expect Chiang to be restored on the China mainland as a result of negotiations? How would the rearmament of Japan affect Russia and China? Or does the West hope to go beyond Russian and Chinese withdrawal and, by the use of nonmilitary pressures, to bring about the overthrow of Stalin and Mao Tse-tung?

Hitherto, fear of the strength attributed to Russia has served to cement the Western coalition. If Russia is revealed to be less powerful than it has been hitherto portrayed, this may require rethinking on the part not only of the United States but also of our allies.

(4) In spite of their criticisms of "containment," Republican spokesmen have repeatedly indicated that they have no desire to rely on military methods except as a last resort, and Eisenhower, while he was in Europe, declared that NATO was an instrument of defense against aggression, not of preventive war against Russia.

On the basis of this record, the Republican Administration would presumably be no more eager to use atomic or hydrogen bombs in a reckless manner than the Democrats, who have not brandished these "unconventional" weapons since Hiroshima and Nagasaki. Assuming that Eisenhower has as much stamina as Truman proved to have during the cold war in resisting extremist pressures, he should be in an even better position than a civilian to block irresponsible action by military advisers. The Republicans, like the Democrats, would still face the problem of how to work out trustworthy *international controls over armaments,* both conventional and unconventional. Should they succeed in this task, the very fact that Eisenhower is personally acquainted with military possibilities and risks would presumably make whatever arrangement he sponsors more acceptable to the American people than if they had been framed by the Democrats. Reorganization and streamlining of the military establishment, both at the Pentagon and at NATO headquarters, may also be effectively carried out by Eisenhower. But a military establishment, no matter how efficient, does not operate in a vacuum. The objectives for which it is used will still remain to be defined. Our recent emphasis on armaments, land and sea bases for atomic attacks on Russia, and the rearmament of Germany and Japan have disturbed our allies, who feel that military expenditures threaten their economic stability, and lend support to Russia's contention that the United States is war-minded.

(5) The emphasis placed by Republican spokesmen on the moral weapons to be used in the struggle of democracy against

communism, and President Eisenhower's own repeated references to a moral "crusade," will focus attention here and abroad on measures short of war which the Republican Administration might use. Among these measures one of the most important is *the expansion of world trade* and, since the United States today is the greatest economic power in the world, this means expansion of our trade with other nations. As a matter of fact, the "dollar gap" between Western Europe and the United States had been considerably narrowed in 1952, being reduced to approximately two billion dollars. This reduction, however, was achieved not by a marked increase in American purchases but by a reduction of European imports, which reduced the total volume of trade and thereby also employment.

The Democrats recognized that this country, far from being self-sufficient, will be increasingly in need of raw materials for both peacetime and wartime needs. They also took steps — through the reciprocal trade program of Cordell Hull which comes up for renewal in mid-1953, through tariff reductions, and other measures — to increase imports and thus give other nations an opportunity to pay with dollars for increased purchases of American goods. The Republicans, by contrast, have hitherto been noted for their attachment to high tariffs, of which the Smoot-Hawley tariff achieved the greatest notoriety. If they persist in this attachment, other nations, no matter how friendly to us or how opposed to communism, will sooner or later turn toward trade with Russia and China, and may even curtail their trade with the United States in retaliation for tariff restrictions on some of their best-selling products.

It will therefore be urgently necessary for Eisenhower to reconstruct Republican thinking on world trade if he is not to lose the support of the NATO countries, as well as of Germany and Japan, which are now reentering world markets with all the more vigor because, unlike the NATO countries, they do not as yet need to use their production facilities for armaments manufacture. This will prove all the more necessary if, as indicated during the election campaign, the Republicans decide to cut down foreign-aid expenditures and substitute long-term loans for outright grants such as were made under the Marshall Plan. The European nations, for their part, want not further aid but trade, offshore purchases, and American investments. Loans, however, must be repaid, and loans, like imports from the United States, must be paid in dollars.

The proposal to coordinate all United States foreign economic activities, now scattered among half a dozen agencies, under a single Overseas Aid Agency, is administratively sound. Such coordination, however, would not answer the question of how countries which continue to receive aid from us, economic or military or both, would be able to pay us for such aid, or how we could hope to obtain from them the raw materials needed for our still expanding industries unless we, in turn, help them to develop their resources with machinery for which they must pay here in dollars. It is therefore encouraging that leading American organizations, including some which once seemed worried about the expansion of imports, like the National Association of Manufacturers, now recognize the need to improve opportunities for sales here by other nations, to simplify customs procedures, to alleviate the rigidities of the "Buy American" program, and to compensate domestic producers who regard themselves as threatened by foreign competition instead of indefinitely protecting them at the expense both of foreign producers and American consumers.

(6) Another important moral weapon is *the development of underdeveloped areas*, whose poverty and desire for rapid improvement have made them peculiarly susceptible to communist propaganda.

Recognizing the efficacy of this weapon, the Democrats

have sought to meet the challenge of communism with the Point Four program and other measures designed to improve economic and social conditions in nonindustrialized nations. But they have run into two important difficulties: first, these nations, if they have themselves recently achieved independence, insist on the grant of independence also to peoples still under Western rule, such as the Tunisians and Moroccans; and second, these nations, whose raw materials once flowed into the industries of the advanced Western powers, now want to use at least a part of their materials for their own economic development and modernization, according to their own ideas of what constitutes a good life.

The Republicans will have to face the same problems as the Democrats in attempting to reconcile the interests of the Western European partners in NATO with those of the colonial peoples and of nations but recently freed from colonial rule. They will also have to respect the desire of underdeveloped nations to build their economies on whatever principles seem best to them, even if this means socialism or communism, provided these nations do not vanish behind the Iron Curtain. The Republicans, more than the Democrats, can be expected to encourage the use of private investments, rather than of government grants, for the development of the Middle East, Asia, Africa, and Latin America. They may prove more generous in giving guarantees to private American investors (although this may seem a contradiction of the spirit of risk-minded free enterprise) and in easing their double tax burdens. But they will be no more able than the Democrats to impose American free enterprise on nations which prefer other patterns of economic development; and no matter how much they might prefer to postpone the further liquidation of colonial empires, they will be no more able than the Democrats to stop the course of fast-moving events. Imperialism is no longer in fashion, and farsighted American businessmen have recognized this, from Nelson Rockefeller in Latin America to Aramco in Saudi Arabia.

A Pacific defense pact, or anti-communist pledges by conservative governments of underdeveloped areas, will not be regarded by the Asian peoples as acceptable substitutes for land reform, improvement of economic and social conditions, attempts at industrialization, and other measures which are now universally regarded as essential to speed the emergence of nonindustrialized nations from economic backwardness and military insecurity. Republicans who have been in the habit of denouncing reforms at home as inspired by "Leftists" may be troubled to find that President Elpidio Quirino of the Philippines regards the land-reform program suggested by American advisers as "Leftist," and apparently prefers to take the risk of continued Huk guerrilla warfare, inspired by land-hunger, even if it gives aid and comfort to communism. The Republicans will thus have to choose between their fear of noncommunist "leftism" as a remedy for communism and their avowed determination to take "positive" action against communism. Either the Republicans do favor "change" in Eastern Europe, Asia, the Middle East, Africa, and Latin America, and must accept the risks that change entails — or they will have to stop talking about "positive" policy. Nor will it be possible for the Republicans, in dealing with the non-white peoples of the world, to continue placating at home advocates of "white supremacy."

(7) While the Republicans will continue to argue that, had it not been for the blindness and fatal weakness of the Democrats, Russia and communism would hardly have made the gains they achieved since World War II, it can hardly be said that since 1947 Democratic spokesmen have been less vigorous than the Republicans in their denunciations of Russia and communism. As McCarthy's accusations of "Commu-

nists in government" mounted in intensity, President Truman and Dean Acheson were driven to adopt policies often indistinguishable from those advocated by their opponents. They castigated the Kremlin's every action; they jettisoned American experts on Asian affairs; they renewed aid to Chiang Kai-shek; they negotiated about military bases and financial assistance with General Franco; they urged all nations to indicate whether they are "with us or against us." It is difficult to see how much further the Republicans can go in this direction unless, as suggested above, they decide to take the risk of open war with Russia by using Chiang's troops or Japanese forces in Korea, bomb Russian territory, encourage the Germans to recover their lands in the East by force, and put weapons into the hands of the Eastern Europeans and the Chinese on the mainland. Such a program, although extraordinarily tempting, is difficult to reconcile with the assertions of Republican spokesmen that they are opposed to preventive war, that the struggle against communism must be won by moral weapons, and that the United States must drastically reduce its defense expenditures. Nor will repudiation of the Yalta and other wartime agreements of itself alter the existing balance of power which these agreements, however repugnant they may be to our moral sense, recognized in the context of their times.

If the Republicans mean what they say, then they will have an admirable opportunity to seek the defeat of Russia and communism not only by a generous economic and financial policy toward nations outside the Iron Curtain but above all by safeguarding and expanding democratic freedoms in the United States as a living example to the peoples of Russia, China, and the Eastern European nations subjected to dictatorship. Assaults, if only verbal, on social achievements won in this country under a Democratic administration, and encroachments on civil liberties, whether fostered by McCarthy or McCarran, will gravely weaken the position of the United States

in the moral struggle against Russia, and will facilitate the task
Stalin set for the Kremlin at the nineteenth Communist party
Congress of October 1952 when he predicted that there would
be no war between the U.S.S.R. and the United States, but
that conflicts would develop between the United States and
the other nations in the anti-communist coalition.

Perhaps the most important contribution the Republican
Administration could make, in the long run, to foreign policy
would be the creation of a bipartisan commission composed of
men and women of national prestige to reconcile the needs of
national security with the growing necessity of preserving and
advancing the basic freedoms whose decline could rapidly deprive the United States not only of democracy at home but of
the opportunity to act as leader of the democratic coalition
against totalitarianism. As long as any American who does not
agree one hundred per cent with a given set of doctrines can
be called "subversive," with all the social and economic consequences such denunciation implies; as long as the word of
self-confessed Communists, who freely admit that they had
been trained to lie, is accepted in preference to that of non-
Communists; as long as past mistakes in judgment or unpopular association can be equated with disloyalty; as long as the trial
of accused persons is entrusted not to the courts but to Congressional committees whose members have no responsibility
for their decisions and enjoy immunity from suit — the United
States will find it increasingly difficult to inspire confidence in
its common sense, its integrity, and its reliability in time of
crisis. Among its tasks, the proposed national commission should
be asked to define the dangers which, it believes, confront
the United States at home and abroad; the remedies for these
dangers; the limits of permissible state interference with basic
freedoms; and the machinery through which such interference
can legally be effected.

That President Eisenhower fully grasped the limits of realities within which the foreign policy of his Administration will have to be carried out was indicated by his Inaugural Address of January 20. Contrary to the predictions of some of his political opponents at home and his critics abroad, he refrained from any statements that might be interpreted as "warmongering." In his nine-point declaration of principles he, who had repeatedly stressed that NATO was not a preventive-war coalition, expressed his abhorrence of war "as a chosen way to balk the purposes of those who threaten us," and said that "the first task of statesmanship" is "to develop the strength that will deter the forces of aggression and promote the conditions of peace. For, as it must be the supreme purpose of all free men, so it must be the dedication of their leaders, to save humanity from preying upon itself." In the light of this principle, he continued, "we stand ready to engage with any and all others in joint effort to remove the causes of mutual fear and distrust among nations, so as to make possible drastic reduction of armaments," provided honesty and good faith in carrying out pledges are observed. At the same time he repudiated appeasement as futile. "Americans, indeed, all free men," he declared, "remember that in the final choice a soldier's pack is not so heavy a burden as a prisoner's chains."

He forswore intervention in the internal affairs of nations, declaring that the United States "shall never use its strength to try to impress upon another people our own cherished political and economic institutions." He called for greater productivity in this country so that the United States can help defend freedom and fulfill its trust in world affairs, and he promised to "foster everywhere, and to practice ourselves, policies that encourage productivity and profitable trade," thereby holding out the promise of a liberalized foreign-trade policy. He emphasized the value of the United Nations; urged the formation of regional groups of "free peoples" within the framework of the UN, notably in Europe; stated that

Americans "hold all continents and peoples in equal regard and honor"; pledged himself to make the United Nations not only "an eloquent symbol but an effective force"; and reiterated that "in our quest for an honorable peace, we shall neither compromise, nor tire, nor ever cease."

Thus the President took the very first opportunity at the beginning of his Administration to proclaim in most solemn fashion his faith in and his dedication to the principles of international cooperation which the American people, in a striking reversal of the isolationist point of view of 1919, have gradually come to accept in the past decade — have indeed accepted to such an extent that Eisenhower's statements, which would have been regarded as revolutionary in 1937, when Franklin D. Roosevelt launched the trial balloon of his "quarantine" speech, are now regarded as truisms. But a man as experienced in military and political affairs as Eisenhower would be the first to admit that the declaration of principles is one thing, and their implementation another.

The ultimate test of the first Republican Administration in twenty years will be the kind of Republicans who will direct its policies. If the conservative group headed by Senator Robert A. Taft of Ohio, who before the inauguration of President Eisenhower expressed satisfaction that the United States could now go back to the days before the New Deal, turns out to be the dominant element, then it will prove increasingly difficult for this country to perform the role of leader in a twentieth-century democratic world community. If the liberal Republicans who, in the first instance, sponsored the nomination of Eisenhower, succeed in taking and holding the helm of national affairs with the support of liberal-minded Democrats, then this country will be in a stronger position than it has been since 1945 to harmonize its policies with those of other nontotalitarian nations.

For if the Republicans can avoid succumbing to the fear of Russia and communism, which some of them fanned during the postwar years and which increasingly beclouded the judgment of the Democrats, they have an unrivaled opportunity to demonstrate to the Russians, as well as to the rest of the world, that a Republican Administration respects the rights of labor, protects and advances the opportunities of our non-white fellow citizens, is ready to help other nations help themselves irrespective of their ideologies provided they are not plotting aggression and subversion, recognizes the revolutionary nature of our times, and does not expect to force the rest of the world into the pattern of life developed in the United States. If the Republicans can do this, they will have won the greatest possible victory over Russia and communism. For they will have demonstrated that capitalism, far from becoming increasingly reactionary and warmongering as predicted by doctrinaire Marxists, can effect a peaceful transition to enlightened economic policy at home and to cooperate with other nations on a basis of equality.

(8) Such cooperation can be most effectively carried out through the *United Nations* which, in spite of some vicious attacks on the very principle of international organization, is supported by Republicans and Democrats. Republicans, more than Democrats, have tended to emphasize untrammeled national sovereignty, and have expressed fears that the United Nations and other international agencies might tamper with the independence of the United States. The Republican Administration now has an opportunity to convince the more lukewarm among its followers that participation in the United Nations, far from diminishing the United States, enriches us through the shared experience of working with other countries for common ends, no matter how different may be the traditions, methods, and national objectives of the member

countries. The Republicans would thus be able to destroy, once and for all, the myth that the party irrevocably suffers from a nostalgia for isolationism.

Before the Republicans can liberate other nations, they must liberate themselves from the fear not merely of Russia and communism, which had also come to dominate the Democrats, but from fear of the changes the twentieth century has wrought within our own borders. A great Republican, Abraham Lincoln, saw this clearly when he said, "In giving freedom to the slaves, we assure freedom to the free." We no longer have slaves in our midst. But as long as we perpetuate or tolerate discriminations and tensions born out of fear of each other, whether based on political, economic, or ideological grounds, none of us can enjoy freedom, nor can we convincingly offer it to other peoples. Repressive policies used by dictatorships are unworthy of American democracy, whether it is led by Republicans or Democrats. Only if we persist in the determination to maintain genuine democracy here can we hope to inject the same determination into foreign policy. As President Eisenhower said in his Inaugural Address, "Whatever America hopes to bring to pass in this world must first come to pass in the heart of America."

France's grand old man, Édouard Herriot, commenting in his autobiography on French policy toward Turkey, says, "France has never had a real republic's foreign policy." The United States, the world's most powerful republic, is still in the process of forging a policy that would accurately reflect the basic ingredients which go into the making of a democracy. The most essential of these ingredients is faith in our own capacity to act democratically. This, and this alone, can make us face the grueling tasks of foreign policy without fear.

INDEX

Date Due